DISSENT AND ORDER IN THE MIDDLE AGES

The Search for Legitimate Authority

Twayne's Studies in
Intellectual and Cultural History

Michael Roth, General Editor
Scripps College and the Claremont Graduate School

DISSENT AND ORDER IN THE MIDDLE AGES

The Search for Legitimate Authority

Jeffrey Burton Russell

Twayne Publishers • *New York*
MAXWELL MACMILLAN CANADA • TORONTO
MAXWELL MACMILLAN INTERNATIONAL • NEW YORK OXFORD
SINGAPORE SYDNEY

Dissent and Order in the Middle Ages:
The Search for Legitimate Authority

Twayne's Studies in Intellectual and Cultural History, No. 3

Twayne Publishers
Macmillan Publishing Company
866 Third Avenue
New York, New York 10022

Maxwell Macmillan Canada, Inc.
1200 Eglinton Avenue East
Suite 200
Don Mills, Ontario M3C 3N1

Macmillan Publishing Company is part of the Maxwell Communication Group of Companies.

10 9 8 7 6 5 4 3 2 1 (hc)
10 9 8 7 6 5 4 3 2 1 (pb)

The paper used in this publication meets the minimum requirements of American National Standard for Information Sciences—Permanence of Paper for Printed Library Materials. ANSI Z3948–1984. ∞ ™

Printed and bound in the United States of America.

Library of Congress Cataloging-in-Publication Data

Russell, Jeffrey Burton.
 Dissent and order in the Middle Ages : the search for legitimate authority / Jeffrey Burton Russell.
  p. cm. — (Twayne's studies in intellectual and cultural history ; no. 3)
 Includes bibliographical references and index.
 ISBN 0-8057-8603-1 (alk. paper) — ISBN 0-8057-8628-7 (pbk. : alk. paper)
 1. Heresies, Christian—History—Middle Ages, 600–1500. 2. Europe—Church history—Middle Ages, 600–1500. I. Title. II. Series.
BT1319.R868 1992
273'.6—dc20
                92-5328
                CIP

For Sherry and Emily

Contents

Foreword

Twayne's Studies in Intellectual and Cultural History consist of brief original studies of major movements in European intellectual and cultural history, emphasizing historical approaches to continuity and change in religion, philosophy, political theory, aesthetics, literature, and science. The series reflects the recent resurgence of innovative contextual as well as theoretical work in these areas, and the more general interest in the historical study of ideas and cultures. It will advance some of the most exciting work in the human sciences as it stimulates further interest in cultural and intellectual history. The books are intended for the educated reader and the serious student; each combines the virtues of accessibility with original interpretations of important topics.

Dissent and Order in the Middle Ages: The Search for Legitimate Authority is a broad survey of the variety of religious expressions in the medieval period. The book examines the dynamic of orthodoxy and heterodoxy from the fifth century through the fifteenth century. Jeffrey Russell's study ranges across the various European responses to the development of Christian beliefs, practices and centers of power. Heresy is shown in the context of the consolidation of doctrine by the Catholic Church, and readers learn how heretics and orthodox leaders existed in relation to one another. The tension between dissent and order created the ideas and institutions which have comprised Christianity throughout its history. By examining this tension, Russell has provided us with an account of how tradition and innovation were interconnected in the religious life of medieval Europe. The book thus provides a history of Christianity's development in European culture as an institution and body of beliefs up to the eve of the Reformation.

Russell's volume is distinguished by the breadth of its survey, and by the ways in which the author connects long-standing historical concerns with contemporary theoretical questions. How do the mainstream and the marginal inform one another, define one another? How did medieval institutions attempt to control the spiritual life of the faithful? How can one know and judge the deepest beliefs of another person? Rather than preserve the binary opposition between the heretics and those against whom they rebel, Jeffrey Russell has given us a nuanced account of the dynamic interrelationship of essential aspects of the cultural history of Christianity.

Michael S. Roth
Scripps College and the
Claremont Graduate School

Preface

I would like to express my gratitude to Penelope Adair, Gillian Ahlgren, Richard Barton, Robert Benson, Alan Bernstein, Courtney Booker, Robert Chazan, Sarah Cline, Peter Diehl, Donald Fleming, Jean French, Frank Gardiner, James Given, Thomas Goodman, Christine Gulish, Anthony Gythiel, Kirsten Hawkins, Marian Hollinger, Scott Jessee, Scott Kenworthy, Gerhart Ladner, Richard Landes, Gavin Langmuir, Robert Lerner, Maria Lichtmann, N. C. Luebben, Douglas Lumsden, Angus Macdonald, Gary Macy, E. Ann Matter, Deborah McBride, R. I. Moore, Barbara Newman, Sharan Newman, Alexander Patschovsky, Edward Peters, Janet Pope, Jill Raitt, Gordon Schaeffer, David Schmidt, Kurt-Viktor Selge, Heather Tanner, Wilfred Theisen, J. M. M. H. Thijssen, Philip Timko, Kristine Utterback, Scott Waugh, and Ulrike Wiethaus.

1

The Concept of Heresy before the Council of Chalcedon (451)

This book investigates the tension between order and dissent in the Christian religion from the time that basic Christian theology was established around the time of the ecumenical[1] Council of Chalcedon in 451 to the eve of the Protestant Reformation in 1500. The book could have been arranged either chronologically or topically; the choice was for a chronological arrangement within which topics are highlighted. Three key concepts are used for the focus and structure. The concepts, broadly defined, are *dissent*, any challenge to prevailing religious views; *order* (sometimes *ecclesiastical order*), those persons or institutions with the power to set prevailing religious views; *authority*, power deemed legitimate because allegedly derived from God.

The thesis is that dissent and order were in frequent tension in medieval Christianity and that this tension was both inevitable and creative. Sociologically, such creative tensions almost inevitably develop in churches, universities, businesses, governments, or other institutions. *Dissent* and *order* are theoretically polar opposites, but the poles are not fixed Platonic ideas but rather are in flux through time and place. *Authority* is also a fluid concept because ideas about what channels God uses to express his will for the Christian community shift.

Furthermore, the topics and categories used in this book are neither static nor precise; rather, they are devices used in order to understand more clearly. Theologians and modern historians both tend to press people or movements into categories in order to make sense of them. This is proper as long as we keep in mind that these categories are intellectual constructs, abstractions that do not detract from the personal real identity of the men and women who thought and acted as participants in this tension, whether as heretics or agents of order.

The Beginning of Heresy

Most books and articles addressing this topic have been called histories of heresy, but this is too narrow an angle of vision. The word *heresy* derives from the Greek *hairein*, "to make a choice (good or bad); hence *hairesis*, an "opinion." By the end of the apostolic age at the beginning of the second century, many Christian leaders came to believe that in order to maintain the coherence of the Christian community, some "opinions" had to be excluded beyond the bounds of the community. By the end of the second century, this community was called the church (*ecclesia*), the united body of Christians led by the bishops. Bishops were formally consecrated by the laying on of hands by other consecrated bishops, in a line extending back to the apostles and ultimately to Christ. This "Apostolic Succession" claimed for the bishops the authority to declare what was correct teaching according to the Bible (the Old and New Testaments) and tradition. In addition to the authority of the bishops was that of the church fathers such as Justin Martyr or Irenaeus, theologians whose ideas were accepted by the Christian community. The authority of the fathers chronologically preceded that of the bishops in that the fathers were widely read, preached, and accepted before the bishops' authority was formalized in the second century. The fathers set the limits beyond which ideas could not go without ceasing to be Christian. Once the bishops' authority was formalized, however, it tended to prevail. The inherent tension between these two sources of authority—bishops and scholars— was to break out repeatedly in the Middle Ages and to become a flash point for heresy.

Ideas acceptable to the bishops and to approved theologians were defined as *orthodox* (correct teaching) and *catholic* (universally held). A popular phrase to define orthodoxy was what was believed *semper, ubique, et ab omnibus,* always, everywhere, and by all. Dissenting ideas were considered *heterodox* (divergent). Heterodox ideas, when defined and condemned by the bishops, were deemed heretical. A *heretic* was a dissenter formally condemned by an accepted ecclesiastical authority. At least that was the theory. In practice, the term *heretic* was often flung to discredit one's enemies; in the Middle Ages a number of popes, bishops, monks, theologians, and laypeople were called *heretics* in loose and virtually meaningless vituperation.

The term *heretic* is distinguished from *infidel*, one who is not Christian at all; *apostate*, one who abandons Christianity; and *schismatic*, one who has true doctrine but does not submit to ecclesiastical order. To these categories must be added a fuzzily defined constellation of surviving paganism and magic that is best termed *folk belief*. This included cures through herbs, rituals, or incantations (often mixed with Christian prayers), curses, fertility rites, and other practices. Some heresies contained elements of folk belief. Most folk belief was undetected or ignored by the authorities; because it was not condemned it could not be heretical. Muslims were usually considered infidels, but from the time of John Damascene (675–749) they were often called heretics and Islam a heresy of Christianity. Jews usually occupied their own category. The Eastern part of Christendom emphasized the distinguishing term *Orthodox* (as in Greek Orthodox), while the Western part emphasized the term *Catholic* (as in Roman Catholic), but both parts always considered themselves to be both catholic and orthodox.

Although the term *Christian* was used as early as the first century, the concept of Christendom, *christianitas* in Latin, was coined by Jerome, a fourth-century church father, to mean the Christian religion and soon came to mean the whole community of believers. Thus *christianitas* was originally close in sense to *ecclesia*. By the ninth century it had acquired a political and corporate sense as well: Charlemagne and his advisers devised an ecclesiology (theory about the nature of the church) in which Christendom was a unified entity ruled by the emperor–or by the emperor and the bishops. An alternative view, that of papal supremacy, had existed in theory since at least the fifth century. But the episcopal-imperial model prevailed until Gregory VII's papal reform movement in the eleventh century successfully inaugurated a period of papal predominance.

In the view of Gregory VII (1073–85) and his chief intellectual adviser Humbert of Silva Candida, Christendom (*ecclesia* and *christianitas*) had the pope at its head and under him the bishops and the entire spiritual hierarchy. Both the laity and the clergy were part of the church, but in Humbert's view, all laypersons, even rulers, were inferior and accountable to the spiritual hierarchy. From the late eleventh century on, the idea of *ecclesia* as community of the faithful and as the mystical body of Christ was replaced by the hierarchical concept of Humbert, thus leading to the common usage today of equating the Church with the hierarchy. Under these conditions, dissent could be aimed at both the spiritual and temporal authorities or against the spiritual leaders specifically.

Histories of heresy as such have always been somewhat wrongheaded, because heresy is not an internally coherent concept, let alone movement, of its own. The best way to understand heresy is in its symbiotic relationship with orthodoxy. Orthodoxy defines heresy, and heresy helps define orthodoxy. Philosophically and practically, the development of heresy is part of the development of orthodoxy. A history of heresy makes sense only as a history of the abiding yet developing tension and dynamic within Christianity.

This tension is similar to that between prophecy and order, between those on the one side who feel the power of the Lord speaking in and through them, even against the opposition of established tradition and authority—and on the other side those who work to keep the Christian community coherent and faithful to the traditional understanding of the words and works of Christ. Some medieval writers defending order considered heresy a Platonic reality, an Idea unchanging from the time of the church fathers to the present. Others saw it as more like the Devil, changing its form and appearance in time and place, while its evil essence—defiance of Christ's Authority on earth—never changed. For some, a mirror image of the orthodox Apostolic Succession from Saint Peter (Simon Peter) showed a heretical "apostolic succession" from Simon Magus (a first-century heretic mentioned in the New Testament). And, of course, whichever side of the theological dispute won became orthodox and their opponents heretics.

In order to obtain a coherent concept of heresy, a modern observer looks at the phenomenon through a complex series of lenses. The first two lenses are modern. The first refracts the historian's personal views; the second the views of one's intellectual environment, including one's professors, one's peers, and the general assumptions of one's culture and age. These two lenses shift slowly in time as the individual grows and society changes.

Then historians must combine a set of medieval lenses with these modern ones. When they look at a medieval document, they encounter a vocabulary the nuances of which are the third lens. The fourth lens consists of the seldom consistent concepts behind the vocabulary. The fifth lens is more like an insect's eye than a lens, for it is the multifaceted uses of vocabulary and concept by different medieval writers in different places. And these medieval lenses also shift in time. Thus for the historian of concepts to get a clear fix on medieval heresy is an extremely sophisticated process. The lenses of modern historiographical interpretation will be examined in the conclusion of the book.

The Creative Tension

The tension between dissent and order is the motor driving the development of Christian thought. Without the constant dialectic among ideas, Christianity would have stagnated and possibly died. Yet, although the tension was necessary and productive, it was also divisive and destructive. The opponents in these controversies often forgot that the greatest of all commandments is to love God and neighbor. Both the dissenters and the defenders of order readily fell into the idolatry of putting their own ideas before love of God or neighbor.

Despite the distortions that both sides introduced, this book is meant as a defense of both dissent and order. Most of the men and women on either side were striving for the truth, many with deep love and desire. Any worldview is an act of faith. The tests of it are coherence, humility, charity, openness, and persistence. The study of medieval dissent and order is only a small part of the search for truth, but here, as in other areas of knowledge, we can watch the human mind and spirit opening ever more widely and deeply to the beauty of reality and the celebration of life. Only a person who does not know how much love and pain is involved in the search for truth can be judgmental of others. The men and women we encounter in this book are our brothers and sisters, neither angels nor demons but as complex and ambiguous as we are. Such evil as occurred in the tension between the two sides—and there was much evil—occurred when an individual or an institution imagined that God had granted them authority to do violence to others. It is the most astounding and least attractive feature of Christianity that so many who claim to be followers of Christ, who condemned all violence done to human beings, should so confidently and with such little hesitation violate his precepts.

Nonetheless, we can understand historically why the Christian community shifted from peaceful resistance against evil to active participation in violence. The first reason lies in the alliance between the community and the Roman state beginning with Constantine's conversion and culminating in the Theodosian Code. Once Christianity called upon the state for help in repressing its opponents, Christianity opened itself to condoning or even encouraging violence. The change also heightened the tensions within Christianity between the forces of order, which tended to favor repression, and those of dissent, which by their nature were more tolerant. The second reason is subtler, but psychologically more powerful. Christians believed that human society was a battleground between God and Satan. As early as the second century a tendency began to identify opponents of the church as enemies of Christ and followers of the Devil. As the forces of order drew the borders of orthodoxy more sharply, the more they defined their opponents as enemies of Christ and of society. The attitude of the orthodox community toward a successful heretical leader can quite soberly be compared to the attitude of a modern community toward a perverted serial murderer: the criminal must be destroyed in order to save society.

Medieval heresy was separated from ancient heresy by the Council of Chalcedon in 451. The date is a convenience, for the efforts of the church fathers at Chalcedon to settle basic theological issues once and for all were not entirely successful. Nonetheless, by 451 the orthodox, catholic position on most basic Christian theology was established. This meant a qualitative difference between ancient and medieval heresy. The struggles between orthodoxy and heresy before 451 were more philosophical and theoretical, involving such questions as the nature of the relationship between the Persons of the Trinity or the identity of Jesus Christ with the Second Person of the Trinity. Still, some ancient heresies were more moral than theoretical, for example Montanism, a widely held belief advocating extreme asceticism (the practice of an austere life); Donatism, which denied the validity of sacraments administered by an immoral priest; and Pelagianism, which claimed that an individual did not need divine grace to attain salvation.

After 451, the tensions, although still sometimes theoretical, shifted gradually from theological abstractions toward questions about humanity's relationship to God. How are we to worship him? What is required of us morally? For example, should we follow the apostolic example of living in voluntary poverty? To what extent does the authority of the clergy rest upon its moral integrity? What is the role of the laity in general and the temporal powers in particular within the church? With some exceptions, ancient heresies were intellectual and medieval heresies were moral. Medieval dissent was concerned with the *practice* of the Christian community as much or more than with its doctrine.

The concept of heresy in the Middle Ages is a concept in the minds of contemporary historians. It was also once a concept in the minds of medieval clergy and theologians. The historian's approach is to define the concept in a way that mediates the ideas and behavior of medieval people in coherent terms comprehensible to modern minds. The excitement—and difficulty—of the history of concepts is that concepts are fluid on both ends: that is, the concept of heresy developed through time in the Middle Ages as theological ideas changed, and the concept of heresy has developed among modern writers as historical ideas have changed.

The history of concepts lies on a spectrum between pure history of ideas and social history. It is closer to history of ideas than to social history, but it recognizes that ideas do not exist in a vacuum and must be understood in their social context. Although much good work is being done on the social side of the question, much more needs to be done. But all types of historians of medieval dissent are limited by the difficulties inherent in the original sources, which are usually sparse, usually biased, and often contradict one another. An example is the case of 1022 discussed in the Document and Commentary.

The history of concepts recognizes that medieval heresy, like any other concept, is not a fixed, unchanging absolute, but a human construct. Looking through the lenses of modern historiographical interpretation reveals that during the four centuries from the Protestant Reformation into the early twentieth century, the main differences were between Catholics and Protestants. For traditional Catholic writers, medieval heretics were sinners who stubbornly held wrong doctrines in defiance of legitimate church authority. For traditional Protestant writers, medieval heretics were forerunners of the Reformation: saints who steadfastly kept true doctrines alive in defiance of illegitimate ecclesiastical tyranny.

In the second half of the nineteenth century, political liberals shifted the grounds and perceived medieval heretics as witnesses, not to Protestant truth, but to intellectual freedom and human rights. Thus, heretics appear in H. C. Lea's anti-medieval *History of the Inquisition of the Middle Ages* (1887) and J. B. Bury's *History of the Freedom of Thought* (1913).[2] Other polemicists found bizarre uses for heresy: Otto Rahn saw the medieval Cathars as martyred forbears of Nazism, and for Karl Kautsky medieval heretics were social revolutionaries who expressed themselves in religious terms because they were ignorant of objective Marxist materialism. Raoul Manselli, the first great twentieth century writer on heresy, considered the imposition of Marxist dogma on the past a gross distortion.[3]

Modern historians continue to have their biases, as varieties of academic correctness replaced confessional dogmatism. Contemporary historians tend to deconstruct the sources in a way that makes the orthodox unsympathetic and the heretic more sympathetic, in the line with modern historians' political ways of thinking. But the opportunity exists to open up and out to a wider understanding of the phenomenon of heresy, especially as historians come to understand more fully the transformational symbiosis between order and dissent. This symbiosis was already in motion as medieval dissent began after the Council of Chalcedon, as the next chapter shows.

2

Early Heresy: from Chalcedon to 1000

The change in emphasis from the more intellectual heresies of the early church to the more social heresies of the Middle Ages was less a break than a gradual transformation from the sixth through the eleventh centuries. A marked decline of dissent also occurred between the sixth century and the eleventh. Doubtless many unobserved heterodoxies existed, particularly among the illiterate, who tended to preserve old pagan customs and beliefs. But few were condemned as heretics. Writing was sparse and few sources have been preserved, so known instances of almost any given intellectual phenomenon diminish in this period. The paucity of the sources reflects the decline of literacy and intellectual activity that is rooted in the decline of political, economic, and ecclesiastical order in the period after the breakup of the Roman Empire in the West during the fifth and sixth centuries.

This explanation is part of the truth, but another one strikes closer to the center. For the 600 years between 450 and 1050, order was so fragmented that it was incapable of formulating a coherent system for identifying heresy by distinguishing orthodoxy from heterodoxy. No one could be defined as a heretic unless an orthodox authority defined him so. Authority ultimately derived from God, but opinion varied widely in time and place, even among the orthodox, as to the media through which God's authority was conveyed to human society.

The Question of Authority

Underneath the struggle between dissent and order lay the question of authority. Christian belief has always rested on four main pillars: tradition, the Bible, personal experience, and reason. All authority ultimately comes from God, but who legitimately mediates that authority to the people? The Bible itself cannot be the sole criterion of authority, for the canon of Scripture was determined over the centuries by the Christian community, and in any case every reading of Scripture is an interpretation. By the second century, the community had placed its faith primarily in Apostolic Succession, the belief that the Holy Spirit guided the bishops as custodians of tradition and guardians of Scripture. Because the authority of the bishops was established before the canon of the New Testament was set, the authority of the New Testament is at least partly dependent upon that of the bishops. When the bishops disagreed, the natural recourse was to a council of bishops, the larger the better: hence the "ecumenical" or "universal" councils of the church that began in 325. In theory, the Holy Spirit protected the councils from serious error, and the decisions of the ecumenical councils were accepted by all orthodox Christians through the Middle Ages. In practice, the Holy Spirit was less predictable than one might hope. The councils were sometimes divided and needed an external authority to resolve their differences and enforce their decrees. For political reasons, that external authority was usually the Roman Emperor. The concept of "separation of church and state" did not exist in any ancient polity. Citizenship and membership in the state religion were inseparable. Thus the emperor deemed it his duty as the repository of religious authority to regulate the church, and this seemed entirely natural to contemporaries.

From the fifth century on, the division between the Western and Eastern halves of the Roman Empire and church grew wider in language, liturgy (public religious celebration, especially the Eucharist), law, culture, and politics. In the East, the emperor, seconded by the patriarch of Constantinople, continued to be the prime authority. In the West, the pope, the bishop of Rome, increasingly claimed the authority to direct the community in preserving, interpreting, and communicating the teaching of Christ, including the Scriptures. In the centuries between 451 and 1000, especially in the West, the question of authority was unsettled; consequently, little coherent orthodoxy was found. Eastern and Western Christendom were at odds throughout the period. In the West, the church had to absorb and assimilate vast numbers of new Celtic, Germanic, and Slavic Christians, who brought with them doctrinal and liturgical peculiarities and magical and cultic practices from their pagan past. The system of dioceses and parishes by which Europe was organized by the eleventh century did not yet exist in the seventh and eighth centuries. The claim to universal authority in the church—whether emperor, councils, or pope—was only dimly felt in outlying areas of Christendom.

Reform Movements and the Rise of Heresy

This state of affairs had changed markedly by the mid–eleventh century. Parishes were established and dioceses defined; bishops' powers expanded; temporal rulers consolidated their territories; monastic houses were reordered. Powerful reform movements began with monastic reform at Cluny in 909 and culminated in the Papal Revolution of the mid–eleventh century. By mid–century the authority of the pope was greatly enhanced by the Papal Reform Movement. The "rise" of heresy was intertwined with the reform movements in the church and with the growth of princely power. The main reason that heresy "arose" in the eleventh century was that ecclesiastical and political organizations had pulled themselves together sufficiently to define orthodoxy, condemn heresy, and prosecute offenders. Heresy was sparse in areas where princely power was strong enough to contain it, as in England and Normandy, but also sparse in border areas such as Spain, Scandinavia, Poland, and Bohemia, where pagans or Muslims still constituted a threat to Christendom. Dissent and heresy appeared most frequently in regions in the middle of the political spectrum, areas such as the Low Countries, the Rhineland, France, and northern Italy.

Orthodoxy and heresy arose together from the eleventh century on. The first formal medieval executions for heresy occurred in 1022, in the context of increasing princely as well as ecclesiastical order. Through most of the previous millennium instances of prosecution had been rare and spasmodic. Executions were always a last resort, because execution deprived the heretic of his or her last chance at repentance and therefore of salvation; they could be justified only as a means of preventing the crime from spreading and bringing other souls to damnation.

Even before the eleventh century, however, the prosecution of heretics had begun to develop. The ecumenical councils and theologians in the fourth and fifth centuries had drawn relatively firm lines between orthodoxy and heresy on a number of critical doctrines. Theologians defined heterodoxy; councils issued formal statements (*conciliar canons*) declaring certain heterodox views heretical.

Formal prosecution of heresy in this early period was usually left to the temporal authorities. It was based on a number of civil laws and law codes after the establishment of Christianity as the official religion of the Roman Empire under Theodosius I (379–395). In 438, the Theodosian Code laid the basis for the prosecution of heretics and pagans, and in 453 the Constitution of the emperors Valentinian III and Marcian made pagans and heretics subject to capital punishment and confiscation of their property, meaning destitution for their families and death for themselves. The *Corpus Juris Civilis* (Code of Civil Law, c. 530–550) of the Emperor Justinian codified these laws, forbidding meetings of heretics and condemning anyone who failed to denounce them.

Chalcedon became the touchstone in distinguishing orthodoxy from dissent. Opinions that had earlier been open options were now either defined in or defined out. It was orthodox to believe that the Father, Son, and Holy Spirit were equally and eternally the same God. Those who held to the previously acceptable doctrine of subordinationism—that the Father preceded the Son and Holy Spirit—were now condemned as Arian heretics. Arianism was named after Arius (c. 250–336), who argued for subordinationism at the First Ecumenical Council of Nicea (325). Arianism gradually faded, although it made a temporary comeback as the religion of many of the Germanic peoples during the fifth, sixth, and seventh centuries. On the nature of Christ, it was orthodox to believe that Jesus Christ is both wholly human and wholly divine and that he is the Son of God in all eternity. Christ is one Person with two Natures. As opposed to this "Chalcedonian" position, two opposite points of view were defined as heretical. The Nestorians (named after Nestorius, d. 451) believed that Christ was two Persons (human and divine) with two Natures (human and divine). The Monophysites (*monos/physis:* one/nature) believed that Christ was only one divine person in one divine nature.

These heresies encouraged others with earlier roots to bloom anew. The Nestorian heresy encouraged Adoptionism, an old theory by which Jesus was born with an entirely human nature but was "adopted" as God at the time of his baptism. On the other side, the Monophysite heresy promoted Docetism, the belief that Christ merely appeared (Greek *dokein*, "to appear") to have a body and so did not really suffer upon the cross. Such ancient heresies did not quickly disappear. The Nestorians fled east into Syria, Iran, India, and eventually as far as Central Asia, where a remnant still endures. The Monophysites, even more tenacious, continued to struggle with the Chalcedonians on an almost equal basis for centuries, during which time several of the Eastern Roman (Byzantine) emperors ruling from Constantinople took their side and attempted to repeal or remodel the Chalcedonian position. An unsuccessful compromise was Monothelitism, a view that Christ has one Person, two Natures, and one Will. The Monophysites and their allies, concentrated in Egypt and Syria, lasted as significant powers in the East until the seventh century, when they yielded easily to Muslim conquerors because of their disgust with the imperial Chalcedonian position; some Monophysites remain today in Egypt, Ethiopia, and Armenia.

When the most influential of the Western church fathers, Saint Augustine (354–430), was a young man he briefly embraced Manicheism, the religion of the followers of Mani (executed in Persia 276/7). This heresy was a combination of earlier religious traditions, including Gnosticism—a late Hebrew and early Christian religious mindset positing an extreme dualism between good and evil, spirit and matter—and Persian Mazdaism or Zoroastrianism. Its fundamental tenet was the belief that the cosmos is a battleground between God and the Devil. God created spirit; the Devil created matter and entrapped human spirits in it; the Manichean's duty was to employ revealed knowledge and ascetic piety to liberate his or her spirit from matter. A variant of this spiritual dualism later reappeared prominently in Western Europe in the twelfth century, but the original Manicheism had lost its influence by the time of Augustine's death.

In his later years, Augustine was more concerned with Pelagianism, a heresy of strongly moral dimensions named after the monk Pelagius (d. c. 420) and ably represented by Pelagius's brilliant and assertive follower Julian of Eclanum (d. 454). The Pelagians emphasized the freedom of the human will to the extent that they believed that a person could by his own efforts and deeds earn the grace necessary to salvation. Augustine, taking harder and harder positions in his struggle against Julian, ended by arguing for complete predestination: a person could not be saved except by the wholly free gift of divine grace, which, when offered, he or she could not refuse. Theologians never resolved this issue, the majority remaining closer to Augustine than to the Pelagians and insisting that grace is a gift, freely given by God, that can no way be earned or merited.

Thus the disputes of late antiquity had already begun to be less abstract and more morally oriented. The sixth and seventh centuries were a period when not only knowledge of theology but also knowledge of methods of investigating theology weakened. Augustinian education, with its emphasis on theology and the liberal arts (arithmetic, astronomy, geometry, music, rhetoric, grammar, and logic), the staple of late antique education, declined in the seventh through tenth centuries. Neither orthodox nor dissenters had the intellectual power to produce the tension that generated heresy.

Apocalyptic

Historians have long accepted the rule that Western Europe saw few heresies in the early medieval period, but Richard Landes has argued that those that existed may have been the products of apocalypticism. Apocalyptic—the view that the world would shortly come to an end—went back to late Hebrew thought and was a strong characteristic of early Christianity. Often it was linked with millenarianism—the belief that the end of the world be either preceded or followed by a thousand-year reign of God on earth. Variations on millenarian thought were virtually infinite. Following Augustine, the Christian community as a whole rejected millenarianism, and when it reappeared from time to time it usually did so as a heresy. Augustine, however, retained apocalyptic thought, and indeed it remains orthodox today to believe that Christ will come again and bring the world to a close. Apocalyptic thought forms a spectrum ranging from the established views represented by Augustine and subsequent orthodox theologians to extreme positions often involved with millenarianism.

Apocalyptic thought was common in early medieval Europe. Many collections of commentaries by the church fathers on the

Book of Revelation existed, commentaries that emphasized the moral meaning of the book. The liturgy of the Frankish church was heavily imbued with apocalyptic imagery, and the Fourth Council of Toledo enjoined priests to preach from Revelation in the liturgical season between Easter and Pentecost. In the ninth and tenth centuries, commentaries on Revelation were even more common. Why this was so is still unclear, but it provides background for the thesis that early medieval heresy was inspired by the Apocalypse.

The heretics of the sixth to the early eleventh centuries may have been apocalyptic or simply eccentric. Two episodes of heresy were reported by the historian Gregory of Tours in the sixth century, and Gregory's *History of the Franks* has a decidedly apocalyptic flavor as a whole.[4] In 587, a man named Desiderius appeared in Tours affecting humility in clothing and diet and claiming to work miraculous cures. Messages were sent him by Saints Peter and Paul, whom he considered his equals. Gullible countryfolk flocked to him. Later, a man from Bourges wandered through southern Gaul wearing animal skins and feigning holiness. He eventually proclaimed himself to be Christ and traveled with a woman who claimed to be his sister and whom he called Mary. Crowds flocked to him for advice and healing, and many followed him as his "apostles." At Le Puy he defied the bishop's authority and was executed. The behavior of these people resembles descriptions of later heretics such as Aldebert so closely that unless these later accounts borrowed from the widely read work of Gregory, the apocalyptic explanation seems at least plausible.

The ninth-century revival of learning encouraged by Charlemagne and his scholar-courtiers such as Alcuin and Theodulf revived the seven liberal arts and spread education from the royal palace school to the cathedral schools in the cities. The revival centered on Latin poetry, prose, and art, especially architecture, and produced a phenomenal number of manuscripts preserving classical works. But with little knowledge of Greek or Greek theology, these scholars had little ability to argue or even to understand theological differences. The main importance of this century to the history of dissent is that precedents for royal and episcopal order were set, precedents that would be fully developed two centuries later.

Two important heresies developed in the East in the eighth and ninth centuries. One was Iconoclasm, a ban on visual representations of God or the saints. Iconoclasm was promoted by the Eastern Emperor Leo III from 726 but finally condemned at the Second Council of Nicea (787). Charlemagne's advisers, misunderstanding the decisions of this council as advocating the worship of images, condemned them at the Council of Frankfurt, which Charlemagne summoned in 794, thereby adding another element to the growing tension between East and West. Meanwhile, on the far eastern borders of the Eastern Empire, in Armenia, flourished the Paulicians, who began as Adoptionists and gradually became dualists under Manichean influence. Paulician views later influenced the Bogomils of Bulgaria and through them Western European dualism.

In the eighth century, an eccentric heretic named Aldebert, using apostolic simplicity in gait, speech, and dress, wandered about the countryside near Soissons in northern France, preaching in the open. His charismatic personality brought him the support of the common people and the displeasure of the bishop. His popularity went to his head, and he claimed that he was worthy of veneration and as a living saint could perform miracles. He claimed a miraculous birth, dedicated chapels to himself, and declared himself the equal of the apostles. To his credulous followers he distributed his hair and nail clippings as holy relics and said that he received written messages delivered by angels from heaven. He was condemned as a heretic by the bishop of Soissons and eventually by Pope Zachary (741–752).

In the ninth century, Theuda (847/8), a charismatic woman, exhibited an opposition to authority similar to Aldebert's a century earlier. She toured the villages around Mainz preaching that she had received a special revelation from the Holy Spirit and proclaiming the imminent end of the world. She was condemned by the archbishop of Mainz for unlicensed and doctrinally unsound preaching. Bishop Claudius of Turin (814–820) preached against the veneration of images, the cult of the saints, pilgrimages, and the authority of the pope. Aldebert, Claudius, and Theuda exemplify the worldview informing early medieval heresy. It was an apocalyptic attitude harking back to the primitive church, as the sources refer to Theuda as a *prophetess*, a term that had disappeared in the second century.

The attitude is one of prophetic dissent. *Prophecy* in the medieval context meant the belief that the Holy Spirit may give an individual the grace to speak forth (Greek *prophēmi*) the word of the Lord. The belief that illumination by the Holy Spirit has more authority than the order fashioned by the bishops and the councils constituted a radical claim to a different basis of authority than that of the established order of the church. The organized church that had established its control by 451 asserted that through the Apostolic Succession the bishops were entrusted with authority by Christ and were aided by the Holy Spirit in preserving and expounding Christ's message. They were the custodians of tradition and of the correct interpretation of the Bible. In the process of establishing their authority, these institutional rulers of the church had little patience with individual experiences of the Holy Spirit and even less for claimed "revelations." But personal experience is an essential element of Christianity, keeping the religion alive, and it could not be repressed. The spirit of prophecy welled up in the prophets of the earliest church, then among the martyrs, and then among the desert monks, who sought to follow the apostolic life enjoined by the New Testament more fully than in ordinary Christian worship. However crudely Alderbert and Theuda expressed the prophetic spirit, they were quickened by this lifeblood of personal illumination.

One controversy of the ninth century echoed ancient theological debates. In France, the powerful Archbishop of Reims, Hincmar (c. 806–882), was supported by the theologian monk of Corbie Paschasius Radbert (c. 790–865) and by the great philosopher John Scottus Eriugena (c. 810–877) against the monk Gottschalk. Gottschalk argued Augustine's predestinarian views in their extreme form, double predestination: in eternity, Christ chooses those he saves and those he does not, thus making free will in effect an illusion.

Eucharistic Controversies

Essentially new was the ninth century discussion of the Eucharist. The Eucharist was the center of Christian worship right from the beginning, but it was something that the church had not attempted to define rationally. Now Paschasius Radbert wrote a treatise *De corpore et sanguine Domini* (*On the Lord's Body and Blood*, c. 831–833), introducing a theology of the Eucharist that was unprecedented but which began discussions that are still alive and will probably never be concluded. Christian belief was always clear that Christ is present when the community consecrates the bread and wine in remembrance of the Last Supper. The action of the community gathering in worship was the essential thing. But when theologians began to reflect upon it rationally, they began to discuss the precise way in which Christ is present in the consecrated bread and wine. One could go to two extremes: to deny the Real Presence of Christ—something that was always considered heretical—and to insist that the bread and wine became Christ physically in a corporeal sense. The church has wrestled with the question over the centuries.

Paschasius was the first to argue for the bread and wine becoming Christ corporeally. Another monk of Corbie, Ratramnus, scandalized by this extreme, took a view close to the other end of the spectrum, emphasizing the Eucharist as a sign to such a degree that the Real Presence became attenuated. Paschasius's view gradually became accepted orthodoxy in a modified form: the Eucharistic body and bread were a sign, but a sign of the Real Presence. Theological efforts to define the nature of the Real Presence more closely became complex and convoluted, and debates raged right down through the Protestant Reformation. As early as 838 the Council of Quierzy condemned Amalarius of Metz for maintaining that the Eucharist was merely allegorical.[5]

That Gottschalk and Amalarius should have been condemned is an important sign that the growth of ecclesiastical order promoted the growth of heresy, for neither of the two issues—predestination or the exact nature of the Real Presence of Christ in the Eucharist—had been or ever would be formally resolved. Hincmar, representing the claims of episcopal order, simply had the power to secure his opponents' condemnation as heretics. Gottschalk died in prison.

Eriugena escaped Hincmar's condemnation by writing theology that was beyond the archbishop's understanding. Eriugena had translated the great sixth-century mystic Pseudo-Dionysius the Areopagite (Denis) and then written his own book, *The Divisions of Nature*, influenced by Denis. He was the only significant Western scholar in the ninth century who commanded the Greek language and Greek philosophical discourse. Later, in the thirteenth century, when his ideas were understood, many were condemned retrospectively.

The tenth century, a period of relapse on the part of both spiritual and temporal authority in the West, produced few heretics, mainly because the orthodox authorities were not perceptive enough to identify, or powerful enough to condemn, any hetero-doxies. It was different in the East. By this time the isolation between the Eastern and Western halves of the old Roman Empire and church was almost complete. The pope in Rome had virtually no authority in the Greek-speaking East, and Greek theologians were little heeded in the West. Social and political conditions in the two areas had grown quite different. While heresy was absent from the West, the East produced a notable heresy, Bogomilism, from the 940s on. The Bogomils were dualists of a Gnostic and Manichean stamp, who may have derived their ideas partly from the dualistic Paulicianism coming through Thrace, although some modern historians now believe that Bogomil theology was originally moderate and became extreme only during its struggles with Byzantine orthodoxy. Bogomilism began in Bulgaria around 940 supposedly with a priest named Bogomil, meaning "God's mercy." It entered Western Europe about 1140, influenced Reformist heretics who already had dualist tendencies, and produced a new Western heresy, Catharism. About 1170, its dualism became more extreme, and some Bogomils came to reject matter as evil and to practice severe asceticism.

The will to repress dissent and the legal means of doing so, though they did not fuse before the eleventh century, began earlier. The will to repress dissent grew with the monastic reform movements whose origins go back to about 900. With the decline in imperial political power in the fifth, sixth, and seventh centuries, civil responsibility for the prosecution of heretics faded. The legal means of repressing heresy shifted toward the spiritual authorities. The Germanic laws that replaced or modified Roman law between 600 and 1000 paid little formal attention to heresy. Canon law—ecclesiastical law based on the decisions of popes and councils—gradually took up the slack. Canons (papal and conciliar decisions) were always respected, but until the sixth century no collection existed to make them handy to use. The earliest collections were made in the fourth century. That composed about 500 by Dionysius Exiguus, containing selected decrees of councils and papal decretals, had great influence in the Western Church. When Charlemagne was trying to bring his empire together in the ninth century, he asked Pope Hadrian I to send him a collection of canons: the document that Hadrian sent in 774 was basically Dionysius's collection supplemented by more papal decretals; it is known as the Dionysio–Hadriana. Charlemagne adopted it for the empire in 802. The bishops now recognized the power of such collections and put together some of their own during the period from 845 to 860. The value of using collections of canon law for the supervision of dioceses was again recognized by Regino of Prüm in his practical collection. Made about 910, it was a precedent for larger and eventually more sophisticated collections later. These became an important foundation for the later legal exclusion of heretics from Christendom.

The period from 451 to 1000 was characterized by the survival of folk practices and by their gradual assimilation into Christianity. Apocalyptic expectations seem to account for most of the popular heresies of the period. The main wellsprings of dissent were now among the uneducated, so that the character of heresy shifted from the theological disputes of the early church to more practical concerns. Formal heresies were scant because the forces of authority and order had declined and were powerless to decide whether given ideas or practices were heretical. This would change in the eleventh century, when both temporal and spiritual institutions of order revived.

3

Reform Heresies: 1000 to 1140

The Impact of Reform

From the beginning of the eleventh century both the variety of heterodox opinions and the condemnation of such opinions as formal heresy increased markedly, beginning with the executions at Orléans in 1022. This stirring of heresy was primarily the result of reform movements in the church. The spirit of reform was to induce the clergy to become less concerned with worldly goods and prestige while at the same time bringing them closer to the concerns of people living ordinary lives in the world. Such clergy became evangelists, teachers of Christ by word and example. From the foundation of the great monastic reform house at Cluny in 909, reform spread rapidly through the monasteries, and since the monasteries had almost a monopoly on education and great moral authority in the period, their reforms shaped the Western church.

The impact of this on heresy was twofold. First, by advocating an ascetic life and return to apostolic simplicity and piety, the spirit of monasticism often opposed the institutional power of the spiritual and temporal powers: the bishops and the princes. Monasticism also had its own history of tension between dissent and order. The new reform monasteries were usually founded by radicals seeking spiritual freedom from institutional organization, yet almost all were eventually co-opted into the organized system. Second, the sense of zeal felt by the reform monks spilled over into society and encouraged a number of laypeople to proclaim that the practice of the apostolic life was more important than obedience to the clergy. Some went so far as to argue that the corrupt clergy who had prepared the way for dissent were more wicked than the dissenters themselves.

Reform can be a movement of order against chaos, abuse of authority, ignorance, and immorality. Or reform can be opposed to any and all structures of order. Frequently antiorder Reformists were either co-opted or suppressed by the forces of order. Some radical reformers, such as founders of monastic orders, came to be revered as saints, while others, either through their own extremism or by the vagaries of politics, were deemed to have passed beyond the limits of orthodoxy. Thus for the eleventh and early twelfth centuries clearly distinguishing between heretical reform and orthodox reform is impossible. They are the same movement in dynamic tension. The radical reformers stimulated a widespread reform of the organizational structure of the church, but the more church order was empowered by its growing moral and intellectual standards, the more it sought to define the boundaries of orthodoxy sharply. Thus reform produced heresies both by stimulating prophetic demands for change and by stimulating organizational demand to control the limits of zeal.

An analogy can be drawn between medieval reform movements and certain modern phenomena. In present–day Latin America, for example, Catholic Liberation Theology attacks corruption in church and state, demanding communal involvement and societal change. Latin American Protestants also attack corruption and offer community involvement, but emphasize individual salvation to the exclusion of communal change. To some medieval dissenters, the reform of the corporate church was too abstract, vague, and long-term a goal; they believed that Christ called for their salvation there and then.

Prosecution of Heresy

About the middle of the eleventh century, when the papacy took the lead of the Reform Movement, Christian order became more aware of and more concerned about dissent. This may have been because paganism had been reduced to vestiges and the community had more energy to devote to demanding orthodoxy. The defeat of paganism activated the sociological phenomenon in which a victorious group, having eliminated external enemies, turns to rid itself of internal dissent. When paganism was rife, the forces of order were obliged to be satisfied with a rough and ready assent to Christianity; as order obtained more control over Christendom, it demanded stricter adherence to orthodox doctrines.

Christianity is not inherently inclined to persecute, yet it was always inclined to marginalize groups that did not conform to the mainstream views of the community, and prosecution had been an aspect of Christianity since the Theodosian Code. Prosecution revived after a fundamental shift in the European social system occurred between the ninth and eleventh centuries, a shift from local kin groups or local feudal bonds to a larger society more remotely ruled. In the ninth century, an effort from a distant authority to attack a person for heresy would have elicited a strong response from his or her lord or kin group; by the eleventh century, the more anonymous, complex society permitted the isolation and prosecution of dissenters.

Still, order's primary mode of dealing with heresy between 1000 and 1140 was on the whole charitable, relying on preaching, debating, and persuading, and only relatively rarely proceeding to prosecution. Collections of canon law for local use, following the pattern of Regino, appeared in this period, notably those of Burchard of Worms (c. 1008–1012), Anselm of Lucca (c. 1080) and Yvo of Chartres (c. 1100). These collections included provisions for defining and suppressing heresy. The decline of Roman law had discouraged definition and prosecution of dissenters, but now, as the study of Roman law revived at schools such as Bologna, coercion gradually returned. Gratian's enormously influential code of canon law, the *Decretum* (1140), which for the first time organized and rationalized canon law, melded Roman law with the authority of the Roman pope to create a powerful machinery for orthodox order (*Decretum*, 23–24).

Against the increasing will to repress dissent, Bishop Wazo of Liège (c. 985–1048) spoke out for tolerance. He used Christ's parable of the wheat and the tares (weeds) to argue that just as the good farmer leaves the weeds to grow with the wheat until he separates them at the harvest, so the church should let dissent grow with orthodoxy until the Lord comes to separate and judge them.

Ironically, the agents of order claimed that order was unchanging, that the truth had been maintained from apostolic times and sealed by the Councils of Nicea and Chalcedon. This meant that order often perceived dissent as "innovation" or "novelty." But the orthodox reformers' theory that they were defending a static truth is historically false, for in reality the Reform Movement changed, or developed, what constituted legitimate theory and practice.

Therefore, the Reform Movement produced two opposite kinds of heresy, that of the overzealous reformers on the "left" of order (the Reformist heretics) and the "underzealous" heretics on the "right" of order (the Reverse heretics). Reverse heretics were people defending positions that had been tolerated (though long condemned in theory) but were no longer acceptable to the Reform popes. When the popes sought to abolish the sale of sacraments or ecclesiastical offices, to enforce the celibacy of the clergy, and to prohibit investiture of bishops by lay princes, many who had been profiting by such arrangements resisted the changes. The popes then defined them as heretics. Those advocating permission to buy and sell offices, for example, were defined as Simoniac heretics, and those willing to tolerate a married priesthood were labeled as Nicolaitist heretics. The pedantic obscurity of the names, which derived from minor references in the New Testament, shows that the reformers had to grope for categories for new heresies that they themselves created by defining them.

The orthodox reform movements of the period were characterized by improvement in the morals and education of the clergy, a struggle to lessen temporal control of the church, and a longing for the simplicity of the apostolic life described in the New Testament. Few avenues were open to lay piety in the early Middle Ages; increasingly from the late eleventh century, this changed: beguins, urban guilds, mendicant tertiaries (laypeople practicing a religious rule while living in the outside world), and itinerant preachers multiplied. Heretical reform had the same characteristics as orthodox reform but pushed past the ill-defined lines where orthodoxy ended.

Typical dissenters from 1000 to 1150, such as Tanchelm, who preached against the corruption of the church in the Low Countries, or the bizarre Breton illiterate Eudo, who considered himself a member of the Trinity, demanded the reform of immoral clergy or their removal from office and argued that the sacraments administered by unworthy clergy were invalid. Sometimes they went further and argued that clergy were not necessary at all. They tended to extreme asceticism, demanded simplicity in food, clothing, and liturgy, looked askance at sexuality, even marriage, condemned private property, and denounced the use of icons, including crosses.

In the West, the efforts of the reformers to define all doctrine and practice as precisely as possible set the papacy against Eastern Orthodox, Jews, Muslims, and heretics. Although Jews and Muslims were considered infidels, the Eastern and Western churches had always been theoretically part of a united, catholic, orthodox community. But strains between East and West had been pronounced since the eighth century, and in 1054 the split became formal with the mutual excommunication of the pope and the patriarch. From 1054 on, each side considered the other schismatic, and Christendom was henceforth divided into Western Catholic and Eastern Orthodox churches.

In the West from about 1050 until the Protestant Reformation, the agents of order were ordinarily able to draw the line between orthodoxy and heterodoxy and to define the latter out of the community's tradition as "heresy." Bishops and councils participated in these definitions, but from the eleventh through the fourteenth centuries final authority was usually exercised by the popes.

Dissenters, whether individuals or small groups, unable to seize institutional authority, devalued tradition and elevated to the highest standard of authority understanding of Scripture conferred upon them personally by the Holy Spirit. The sources are generally opaque concerning their personal motivations. To what extent, for example, did sheer boredom, the desire to see a new face, prompt townspeople to rush out to hear a wandering preacher? At what point did a personal belief varying from the social norm begin to threaten other people, who then called upon order to suppress it? Did the dissenters perceive themselves as defying order or merely as seeking an authority beyond order?

Other questions arise about the attitude of people toward heterodox neighbors. In a small community, people have a tendency to protect their friends. This is why inquisitors later in the thirteenth and fourteenth centuries took pains to question individuals carefully and separately. Still, most illiterate people would have had only vague ideas of orthodoxy and heterodoxy, and all but the most ruthless inquisitors were willing to accept the difference between ignorance and heresy.

On the other hand, contemporary medieval writers about the heresies were nearly all literate clerics, and their attitude toward "the people" is generally denigrating. The *populus* was fickle, rushing now to embrace one heretic, rushing again to burn another. The clergy built a dichotomy between *clerici* (clergy) and *laici* (laypeople), and tended to identify *laicus* with *populus* and even with *rusticus* (a hick). Of course, they had to exclude the lay princes upon whose support they relied. Thus *the people* became a term for illiterate commoners. With the rise of urban literacy in the eleventh and twelfth centuries, *populus* and particularly *rusticus* were common insults applied to dissenters. The organizational powers of the Reform papacy after 1050 built upon these assumptions and firmly established the church as a society divided into clergy and laity with the clergy on top.

Eleventh- and twelfth-century heretics tended to differ from earlier medieval heretics in having coherent doctrines (in contrast to Theuda and Aldebert) and in having communities of followers (mostly small but sometimes substantial). The heresiarch claimed an illumination from the Holy Spirit about the meaning of Scripture. So these "textual communities" placed authority in the charisma of their leaders, and secondarily in the Bible (or at least the New Testament) as interpreted by their leaders. The term *textual community* does not imply that its members were literate (other than the leader), only that they respected the literacy of their leader, and they respected his literacy because they relied upon his charisma. The charismatic leader's rendering of the text, rather than the text itself, was the source of authority. The increasing complexity of society in the eleventh and twelfth centuries, the growth of towns for example, may have driven people to seek simple, coherent, and supportive communities. This was true later in the twelfth century of weavers and other industrial employees. Under such circumstances, the people preferred their own leaders, to whom they could personally relate, over the normal organization of the church with its distant bishops and priests.

The Problem of Preaching

Preaching was an important problem. The liturgy was entirely in Latin and therefore intelligible only to the few members of the community who were literate (sometimes even the priests did not understand the words they uttered). Efforts as early as the ninth century had been made to remedy this, using both Latin and vernacular versions of some common prayers and of the Scriptural readings appointed for the day. But the homily or sermon was the chief means by which the people were educated. As early as 813, Charlemagne ordered preaching in the Germanic or Romance vernaculars. The intellectual and pastoral content of the preaching was often quite high, but legal and conciliar injunctions that priests *at least* convey to congregations that God is a Trinity and Christ the Son of the Father indicate that it was also often quite elementary.

From the eleventh century, as part of the Reform Movement, there was a strong emphasis on preaching intelligible and useful sermons to congregations, and the number of books of sermons or of *exempla* (passages or stories to be used in sermons) multiplied. Still, the demand for preaching outgrew the normal clergy's ability to meet it, and so numbers of itinerant preachers began to move from town to town, delivering sermons that were charismatic, often scripturally rich, and sometimes Reformist. Although general suspicions about wandering preachers went back to the second century, medieval bishops might welcome such preachers for a brief stay in order to encourage the people, but they were unlikely to encourage these preachers to linger because of the potential danger of undermining the bishops' authority and respect. Certainly a wandering preacher whose sermons were preferred to those of the local clergy was likely to be an object of envy. In some instances, people left town to follow the preachers, thereby forming the nucleus of a sect; in other situations, converts remained in town to keep the leader's views alive. In either case, the established clergy might initially view the new preachers as a blessing but eventually as a threat to the authority of the established ecclesiastical order. The problem was compounded by the fact that no standard catechism for children or adults existed. All this added up to a threat to the established order.

At first, examples of the new kind of dissent were isolated. At Orléans about 1015 a small group of 20 heretics, some canons of

Sainte-Croix (secular priests attached to the cathedral) and some laypeople, came to light. In 1022, they were condemned by order of King Robert II of France and executed. Their beliefs in many ways resembled orthodox reform. The sources are so diverse and contaminated that a coherent reconstruction of their doctrines is impossible.[6]

Heresy and Social Change

The rise of heresy in the early eleventh century was less the result of an old elite defending itself against new forces than of a new elite—a newly formalized ecclesiastical hierarchy—arising and excluding its rivals. The elite feared growing popular literacy because literacy was slowly becoming a source of power in society as a whole—in business, law, and politics, as well as among theologians. The rise of heresy does not correlate exactly with the rise of literacy, but they are connected because both are rooted in a profound change of society owing to the growth of cities and of a whole new social order based upon this urban revolution. The urban revolution encouraged the formation both of elites and of textual communities, which, under the leadership of charismatic preachers, could become heretical sects.

Heretics appearing at Liège and Arras in 1025, possibly illiterate or semiliterate townspeople, had learned from an Italian named Gundulf a doctrine that rejected baptism and challenged the Eucharist, the two central sacraments of Christianity. Their view that sacraments were invalid when performed by morally unworthy clergy was the first instance of medieval Donatism. These heretics argued not only against the decoration of churches and the veneration of the Cross but also against any use of church buildings. Their authority was the "justice" placed in their hearts by the Holy Spirit, by which they meant a simple way of life dedicated to manual labor and helping one another. Other groups held similar ideas, the common theme being the authority of the Holy Spirit as expressed in the Bible and in the hearts of believers rather than the institutional authority of the bishops and priests. These groups foreshadowed the widespread growth of antisacerdotal (antipriestly) heresy in the next century.

Antisacerdotal heresy could be tied in with intellectual heresy as well. Precedents for intellectual heresy in the Middle Ages went back to the ninth-century debate over predestination. In the mid-eleventh century, the monk Berengar of Tours (c. 1010–1088) debated the nature of the Eucharist with Archbishop Lanfranc of Canterbury. Berengar took a complex view of the Eucharist, employing Aristotelian analyses and raising the debate to a new level of sophistication. Berengar seems less to have denied the presence of Christ's Body and Blood in the Eucharist than to have opposed crude formulations of the doctrine. But Lanfranc and his other opponents claimed that he denied the Real Presence, and during the rest of the Middle Ages Eucharistic errors tended to be condemned as "Berengarian."[7] Lanfranc and the early scholastics argued that some change (however defined) in the bread and wine took place at the consecration. Personal and political concerns were not lacking here, as in most cases, for Lanfranc was a Norman opposed to the Angevin Berengar. The connection of this intellectual debate with the heresies at Liège and Arras is the connection between Eucharistic and antisacerdotal heresy.

Eucharistic heresy is one of the most common themes in medieval dissent. In some instances, the accounts of the heresies are simply garbled and false; in other instances, the heretics misunderstood orthodox doctrine (hardly surprising because it was not only complex but constantly in flux); in yet others, the heretics deliberately attacked the Eucharist in order to attack the authority of the clergy. The chief function of priests was to consecrate the Eucharist; if there was no need for the Eucharist, priests were not needed, or, in an alternate scenario, if anyone could consecrate the Eucharist, priests were equally not needed.

These dissenters could not be tolerated by the bishops without authorizing the fission and atomization of the church. The dissenters' denial of the sacraments and of apostolic authority was a denial of the very bases of Christian tradition. What explains the tendency of these groups to press their ideas of reform so far? Corruption tainted some of the clergy, but it always had. What was new was the growth of towns and commerce, producing an urban population with enough literacy to read the Bible or at least to grasp the Scriptural interpretations offered by the charismatic leaders of textual groups. The bishops' efforts to control such groups and bring them into line sometimes succeeded but often provoked the dissenters to more extreme views as they lost their trust in ecclesiastical order. This, in turn, led to bishops' formally condemning them as heretics.

The attitudes of the heretics toward the established clergy were equally intricate. Most heretical groups began by thinking of themselves as Catholics. In some cases, their sense of corporate identity with Catholicism was broken, and they assumed other corporate identities. This was clear with the Cathars later; in this earlier period the degree to which the dissenters continued to consider themselves Catholic is unclear. It is also unclear to what extent charismatic leaders of dissent were introducing novelties (a term that in theology was always pejorative, because it implied adding something to the essential message of Christ and the apostles), or whether they were merely articulating concerns that the community had already felt but had been unable to enunciate.

The clergy had dominated the education and religion of the early Middle Ages because of their near monopoly of learning and texts. Now they were tightening control of doctrine. But at the same time new urban classes were appearing with enough knowledge to challenge this domination. Dynamic changes were also taking place in the twelfth-century countryside, but it was in the cities and along the trade routes between them that the propagation and dissemination of dissent was strongest.

A complex example of the dynamic was the movement of the Pataria in Milan, one of the largest and most populous cities of the period. Ariald, a deacon, began the Pataria in 1057 by preaching against clerical immorality. The Patarenes held some heterodox views, but they were not condemned as heretics. The Pataria was primarily a social and political movement, illustrating how in an increasingly complex, urban, literate society, religion itself became inextricably a part of that complex. The parties shifted with kaleidoscopic rapidity, and the course of the dispute is too long to trace. The political elements included the power of the pope, the power of the emperor, the power of the archbishop, the power of the upper clergy, the power of the civic authorities in Milan headed by the knightly class, and the power of the hitherto repressed urban poor. The Patarenes extended their influence to other cities in northern Italy and remained an important element of Italian politics and religion from 1050 to 1075.

In its religious aspect, the Pataria was a movement of extreme, "overzealous" reform. It was supported by many of the urban poor and by the some of the uncorrupt lower clergy, but it was led by two knights, Erlembald and Landulf. They denounced the corruptions of the higher clergy—wealth, buying and selling offices and sacraments, and clerical marriage—and called for a boycott of the churches and the sacraments of such clergy. The higher clergy responded by accusing the Patarenes of heresy, but Popes Alexander II and Gregory VII, eager to repress Simoniacs and Nicolaitists, instead supported the Pataria. Nonetheless, the sources report Patarene ideas that went beyond what the popes could tolerate: Landulf preached without authorization and told the people they should despise the churches of the higher clergy as if they were barns; Erlembald practiced as a priest even though he was never ordained. Even radical orthodox reformers such as Peter Damian (1007–72) warned that the Patarenes were going too far. But because the practical definition of heresy at this time was what the pope said it was, and the pope did not formally condemn them, the Patarenes technically were not heretics.

The urban poor supported the Pataria out of economic as much as religious resentment. Quite another aspect of poverty came to the fore at the beginning of the twelfth century: poverty chosen voluntarily in order to imitate Christ and the apostles. The context again was the growing prosperity and wealth of the towns, which was creating new classes of wealthy people. Such people were the target of envy, but as the urban middle class became richer, some of them, like many previous monastic leaders, were struck by the dissonance of their way of life from that of the apostles. They accepted poverty for themselves and preached it to others in imitation of Christ.

Papal support for the Patarenes seems to have declined as the papal political agenda no longer had use for them. Then, though the Patarenes had never been condemned as heretics, the term *patarene* along with *beguin* gradually became a common noun for *heretic*.

Voluntary Poverty

The roots of the movements of voluntary poverty go back to the Gospels and the Acts of the Apostles by immediate way of the revived monastic ideals of the eleventh and twelfth centuries, when a great number of new ascetic monastic orders were founded, the most prominent of which were the Cistercians and Carthusians. The ascetic spirit flowed beyond the monastic walls, and a new kind of religious order came into being, the regular canons, imbued with the monastic spirit and semimonastic rules, while at the same time dedicated to living in urban communities and preaching to the public. These new orders of canons were approved by the papacy, among them the Premonstratensians, the Victorines, and the Augustinians.

Some zealous ascetics, such as Robert of Arbrissel and Bernard of Tiron, refused to live in any community or under any rule. Dressing roughly, they went about in the forests and from village to village, relying on charity for their living and preaching the gospel of simplicity and service. The ecclesiastical establishment had a brief opportunity to take heed and to make a radical move that could have changed the history of Christianity. Pope Paschal II (1099–1118), influenced by voluntary poverty—and pressured violently by the emperor—declared that the church should divest itself of all worldly possessions and power, a view that would later be promoted by Wyclif as *disendowment*. It was not a view that the twelfth-century ecclesiastical establishment took seriously for any length of time.

Zeal for poverty, kindled by the Holy Spirit and unrestrained by order, could pass into heterodoxy and eventually be condemned as heresy. Peter of Bruys (d. 1140) and Henry of Lausanne (d. c. 1145) were wandering preachers who were condemned. They differed from Robert and Bernard in doctrine and practice, but one of the reasons why they were condemned and the others not was that they lacked the protection of powerful noble patrons such as Robert enjoyed.

Henry was born in Lausanne; his first known preaching activity was at Le Mans, although he must have been active earlier, for he already had followers when he entered that city. He arrived at Le Mans in 1116 just as the distinguished bishop, Hildebert of Lavardin, was about to depart on a visit to Rome. Hildebert had long been an ardent reformer and a patron of Robert of Arbrissel, whom he thought Henry resembled. Hildebert and Henry saw one another as fellow reformers. Henry had a reputation for reformist zeal, for excellent preaching, and for reliable character, so when he arrived during Lent the bishop welcomed him and confidently left town.

The sources for the events that followed are varied and must be taken critically. Some were composed by clerical friends of the bishop and portrayed Henry as a licentious pervert, an accusation contradicted by their own admission that people flocked to him because of his great piety and holiness of life. The hostility of the established clergy to such a dissenter, coming into town and upstaging them, was natural. Their best defense was to accuse the dissenter of hypocrisy. Because Henry's personal piety, along with his charisma, was what attracted the people, his opponents undermined this perception with accusations of gross immorality. Another, literary, element was involved in such accusations as well. To the "realist," Platonic, theological mind, a heretic was a heretic; heresy was one coherent phenomenon that merely changed its appearance and form. Therefore, because the early fathers accused the early heretics of gross immorality, modern heretics must be equally gross.

Henry may have been encouraged by Hildebert's warm reception to go farther than he otherwise might have. He thought of himself not as a heretic but as a reformer. His zeal in preaching against the corruption and wealth of the clergy stirred up popular antagonism against both priests and bishop, and when Hildebert returned from his journey he was greeted by a mob that pelted him with filth, shouting "Go bless the mud; we have a father [Henry, or more likely, the Holy Spirit] greater than you." Hildebert tried to reason with Henry and bring him under the control of apostolic authority, but now Henry claimed to be responsible, not to the bishop, but directly to God. It is unclear whether he rejected Apostolic Succession; he did not deny the priesthood but argued that only worthy priests could consecrate the Eucharist. He denied that marriage was a sacrament needing clerical blessing and dismissed the need to confess to a priest,[8] and he rejected the baptism of infants, reserving that sacrament to those old enough to know what responsibility they were assuming.

Hildebert felt that his trust in Henry had been misplaced. A fellow reformer had become a subverter of authority. But in order to condemn Henry, Hildebert had to reflect consciously upon the nature of Henry's offense. It was not just that Henry challenged the bishop—this might sometimes be legitimate, after all, if the bishop were sinful or incompetent; Hildebert had to demonstrate his own superiority to Henry by showing that Henry was ignorant in theological and liturgical matters. This demonstration, successful though it was, clearly did not sway Henry's supporters, but it gave the bishop a secure theoretical position. He excommunicated Henry and expelled him from his diocese. Henry continued to preach in various places in central and southern France, still gathering followers. He was finally condemned as a heretic by Innocent II at the Council of Pisa in 1135. In effect, by spurning the bishops' authority Henry defined *himself* as a heretic.

Henry was not only a heretic but a *heresiarch*, a leader of heretics, which was morally much worse in the eyes of ecclesiastical order. The agents of order were most likely to declare movements heretical when a charismatic individual attracted a following preferring his authority to that of the established ecclesiastical leaders. An individual keeping unorthodox ideas to himself was unlikely to be condemned as a heretic, although in the medieval church it is unlikely that any individual who felt he or she had a special truth would keep it quiet; he or she would feel drawn by apostolic example to preach it. Still, what was taught need not have been seriously unorthodox to attract the condemnation of the agents of order. The mere fact that the new preacher was preferred to the local clergy was often enough to earn him condemnation. That itself led the ecclesiastical establishment to attribute heretical views to the dissenters and the dissenters to adopt heretical views out of disgust with established order.

Henry's contemporary Peter of Bruys also tended to define himself as a heretic by his rejection of established authority. Born in the Provençal Alps, Peter preached in the mountains until the bishops there drove him out, after which he attracted large crowds at Narbonne and neighboring cities. He denied the authority of the bishops and the institution of the priesthood. The Last Supper was a unique event, and Christ did not intend its enactment in the Eucharist, so that a priesthood was doubly unnecessary. The Petrobrusians (Peter's followers) showed their contempt for the Eucharist and for tradition by openly eating meat on Good Friday. Churches, too, were unnecessary, for Christians could worship in a tavern, street, or stable, as well as in a building of wood or stone. Confessions were not to be made to priests, prayers for the dead were to be eschewed, sacred ornaments were to be destroyed (especially crosses, which only portrayed Christ's torment), and infants were not to be baptized.

If the Eucharist was not the center of Christianity, if the priesthood was invalid, if the bishops' authority was illegitimate, if the tradition preserved by theologians and councils was useless, where did authority come from? From the personal inspiration of the Holy Spirit, and, more dangerous to order, from the charisma of figures such as Henry or Peter who claimed to have that inspiration and to mediate it to their followers. Underlying the heresy of Peter and Henry was the spreading assumption that with the Holy Spirit as its guide, the church had no need of a structure of order, no need for bishops, abbots, or priests. The twelfth century saw a shift from shame (fear of offending society) to guilt (fear of offending God and/or internal conscience), accompanied by a tendency to emphasize individual salvation. This tendency appears in the growing objection to infant baptism on the grounds that an individual ought to know what he or she is doing before being inducted into the Christian community, in the increase of individual prayers to saints, and in the revival of fears that no spiritual benefit could derive from sacraments administered by unworthy clergy.

Such dissenting ideas were most attractive in the towns and cities, where the upper classes were increasingly literate, read parts of the Bible (such as the Psalms) devotionally, and were impatient of ecclesiastical influence in urban politics. The ideas of Peter and Henry were less a coherent theology than an angry rejection of authority, even the authority of Reform bishops and popes. They rejected order and emphasized the inner inspiration of the Holy Spirit. Yet ironically and inevitably, as the heretics drew in followers, they became leaders of sects. The charismatic figure—Peter or Henry—became leader of a textual community, a group centered on the Bible as read and interpreted by its leader. Thus did individual religion quickly metamorphose into something resembling the organized religion that the dissenters deplored.

In the 1130s, Arnold, a regular canon of Brescia, a city that had in the previous century been influenced by the Patarenes, created a political commune in that city; among his programs was the drastic reform of the clergy. He argued that the church should be devoted to apostolic poverty and should divest itself of its wealth and political power. He used the power of the commune to enforce his program. He was condemned by Pope Innocent II at the Second Lateran Council in 1139. Fearlessly, he proceeded to attack the most influential reform leader of the time, Bernard of Clairvaux. Temporarily reconciled with the papacy in 1146, he broke with it again when he became disgusted by the corruption of the leading clergy of Rome. He used his charismatic leadership to drive the pope out of Rome and to declare a republic there. His political and military activities against the papacy led finally to his arrest and execution in 1155 by Pope Hadrian IV.

Arnold was the prophet as politician. His plan for the spiritual authorities to renounce their wealth and power was one of the most radical of the Middle Ages. It constituted rejection of the alliance with wealth and power that the church had maintained ever since it gained imperial power under Theodosius. Unlike the Reform popes, bishops, or even abbots, who believed that they needed power to reform the church, Arnold argued that only by renouncing power altogether could the church escape its involvement in political and economic affairs and thereby liberate itself from temporal control so as to fulfill the apostolic ideal.

Peter Abelard (1079–1142), although he had been one of Arnold's teachers, was condemned on intellectual rather than social grounds. Unlike earlier intellectual heretics, Abelard was condemned almost entirely for political and personal reasons. His was a strange case: he was a heretic without being heterodox. Abelard antagonized ecclesiastical order and especially the politically powerful Bernard of Clairvaux. He was contentious and arrogant as well as brilliant and original, and Bernard and other enemies contrived the condemnation of certain of his ideas at Soissons in 1121 and again at Sens in 1140. Abelard was scholastic in his orientation; Bernard, monastic. But it was ironic that Abelard's claim to be able to achieve truth (and therefore authority) through reason angered Bernard, because Bernard behaved as if the Holy Spirit had given custody of the truth to himself. Thus, Bernard himself had one characteristic of a dissenter: confidence in his own illumination and righteousness along with determination to make others yield to what he knew to be the truth. That he became the saint and Abelard the heretic had more to do with the difference in their political influence than with their theology.

To Bernard, Abelard symbolized a new intellectual spirit coming to dominate Western Europe in the twelfth century. This new spirit, scholasticism, affected philosophy, theology, law, medicine, and epistemology itself. The sources of Christian authority are the Bible, tradition, experience, and reason; Abelard, one of the first scholastics, pressed the claims of reason to a degree new in his time. His lasting, entirely orthodox, theological contributions to the theory of sin and to the theory of the incarnation were matched by his most famous treatise, *Sic et Non* (*Yes and No*), equally orthodox, which presented passages from the fathers showing contradictions among them. Abelard argued that the disagreements could be resolved by recourse to Scripture. He was acutely aware that some passages of Scripture also seem to contradict one another, but he took Scripture as infallible; its contradictions were only apparent and could be reconciled by the use of dialectical reasoning to get at the intentions of the authors, as well as by the traditional method of interpreting Scripture on many levels.

The battle between Abelard and Bernard raises essential points about charisma. Both men were intensely charismatic, each attracting enthusiastic, almost fanatical followings. Yet one figure became a revered saint, the other a kind of intellectual outlaw. The difference cannot reside solely in the irregularity of Abelard's personal life, for Augustine, Francis, and other saints had at one time led unsaintly lives. What made the difference? What made Bernard acceptable to the Christian community and Abelard unacceptable? The question is answerable only in terms of who speaks for the community, that is to say, in terms of authority. Bernard's political allies were established scholars, ecclesiastical and civil leaders, popes. Bernard always subjected his charisma to authority whereas Abelard rebelled against it. Something in Bernard knew not only when to yield to authority but also when to command it. It was he who, relying on the discernment granted him by the Holy Spirit to distinguish the true pope in the schism between Innocent II and Anacletus II, carried Christian society with him in approving Innocent as pope. Abelard had a personality that used charisma defiantly; he had what later theologians would describe as *superbia* (sinful pride) brought on by *curiositas* (vain desire for knowledge). Bernard, like Francis, had a personality that ably wielded charisma in a way that influenced rather than alienated the ecclesiastical structure.

Intellectual Dissent

The growth of rationalism and its efforts to define the truth by deduction produced a resurgence of intellectual dissent in the twelfth century. Heterodoxies arose for two reasons: first, rational theologians thinking rationally often disagree, sometimes to the point of condemning others' arguments as heretical; second, the increasingly strict definition of truth and orthodoxy produced increasing intolerance of unusual ideas. Thus Abelard and Gilbert de la Porrée, both original and brilliant theologians, were condemned for heresy in the 1140s largely because they seemed to oppose the definitions of orthodoxy proposed by Bernard. By attempting to establish the truth exactly, the scholastics established standards and built walls that defined more and more people out of the Christian community as heretical. Given the growth of power on the part of papacy and princes, these rigid standards also guaranteed further prosecutions for heresy.

The dialectical method became the hallmark of scholastic thought in all fields, including theology. Scholasticism was influenced both by Aristotle and by Plato, and some scholastics embraced Realism, the Platonic notion that ideas were eternal and real in eternity. The professors teaching in the cathedral schools (later universities) began to challenge episcopal authority by the use of reason. The condemnation of Abelard raised an important question of how much authority reason was to have vis-à-vis tradition. Against the episcopal order two separate challenges were now set: the challenge of internal illumination and the challenge of natural reason. Now philosophers and theologians were asserting the ability of their own reason to distinguish and interpret Scripture, the fathers, and canon law.

The revelations of the Old and New Testaments are essentially nonrational. Whether they are regarded as divine communications or as merely human myths, there is no rational way to test them, for they were not constructed for use in a rational system. Nonrational systems of thought can be entirely valid. *Nonrational* does not mean *irrational*. An argument can fairly be called irrational only when it violates rationality from within a system intended to be rational. Scholastic efforts to force multivalent nonrational biblical symbols into a rational, dialectical set of categories produced increasingly complex and precarious intellectual structures. The reaction of the bishops to Abelard, though provoked by his personality, symbolized the ancient and inherent tension between reason and tradition as sources of authority.

Because the dominant professors of law, theology, philosophy in the twelfth and thirteenth centuries were eager to construct perfect rational systems, they tended to dismiss nonrationalist thinking as irrationality. By repressing their own nonrationalist tendencies, they unconsciously projected them upon dissenters. Gavin Langmuir argues that as rational definitions became more and more complex, they raised doubts in the minds of the faithful.

The Beginnings of Antisemitism

Doubts and projections did much harm to heretics and even greater harm to Jews. Jews had always been in a special category for Christians. On the one hand, they were respected as God's chosen people to whom the Old Covenant had been given; on the other hand they were condemned for having rejected the New Covenant. From the twelfth century, Christians began to project upon Jews criminal fantasies that were *ir*rational, because it was observable and recognizable that Jews did *not* engage in such crimes, yet people insisted that they did because they *wished* to believe that Jews (like Muslims and heretics) were part of an organized plot of Satan against Christian society.

Antisemitism was relatively new in the late eleventh and early twelfth centuries. Its remote origins go back to the religious antijudaism of some Christians in the early church. But real antisemitism—ethnic antipathy to Jews—became significant in the late eleventh century, becoming an established belief only in the fifteenth century. In the early Middle Ages before 1050, Christians and Jews usually got along reasonably well. Beginning in the eleventh century, this began to change, mostly because of the urge of Reform popes and lawyers to define a visible society of the saved and to define out of that society those who did not submit to the order controlled by popes and bishops. The wall erected between the followers of Christ inside and the enemies of Christ outside became thicker, harder, and more sternly guarded. Intolerance of those who were defined out was expressed in an increasing disposition to condemn and prosecute both infidels and heretics.

A striking difference existed between violent action against Jews and against heretics. Whereas violence against heretics was more often provoked by the agents of order than by the mob, it was mobs who usually rose against the Jews, often in defiance of pleas for tolerance from the bishops. The first sign was in northern France and Germany in 1010–1012, when a rumor spread that a mysterious king of Babylon had destroyed the Holy Sepulchre, the Tomb of Christ in Jerusalem. This provoked popular attacks on Jewish communities in European towns. With quickening urban growth, Jews had found it possible to move into the towns and cities, where they could form their own communities instead of living isolated in the countryside. This made them more identifiable and therefore more vulnerable. Their success at trade also made them the object of envy. In Rome during 1020 and 1021, Jews were accused of mocking the crucifix and were beaten. It was not until the doctrinal controversy over the Eucharist between Berengar and Lanfranc deepened concern about the true nature of the Eucharist—in what way the bread and wine were transformed into the Body and Blood of Christ—that accusations that Jews desecrated the Eucharist began.

The tendency in Christian culture from the late eleventh century to emphasize the physical, human suffering of Christ on the cross added fuel to the illusion that Jews would steal and torture the Eucharistic Host. The irrationality of this Christian belief is of course profound. The Jews obviously did not believe that the Eucharist was Christ, so why should they trouble to degrade it? To show their contempt for Christendom or (as a more sinister answer gradually emerged) to serve their master, the Devil. In 1063, knights on the way to crusade in Spain attacked several Jewish communities in southern France. In the first half of the eleventh century began the custom of administering a ritual blow to a Jew outside church on Easter in punishment for "the Jews'" responsibility for the crucifixion.

After Urban II preached the First Crusade against the Muslims in 1095, many crusaders felt that it was simpler to attack infidels closer to home. After all, virtually no Muslims lived in Europe north of the Pyrenees. In 1096 Jews were rounded up in the Rhineland and France, and those who did not convert were put to the sword. Earlier incidents of brutality had been on a small scale, but those of 1096 involved the massacre of hundreds and set a hideous precedent. The Second Crusade in 1146 provoked more violence, especially in the Rhineland, and it was checked only by the passionate preaching of Bernard of Clairvaux himself. Bishops often intervened to prevent violence, and Christian theologians argued that the Jews as God's People of the Old Covenant should be given special respect. In 1179, the Third Lateran Council decreed that Jews were to be protected from beatings and cemetery violations and that their property should not be confiscated unless for just cause and by due process.

Nonetheless, partly because of the papal reformers and partly in defiance of them, the stereotype of the evil Jew, the outsider, the plotter, the enemy of the Holy Places, the rich exploiter of the poor, was widely established in the popular mind in the twelfth century.

Beliefs grew more lurid. In 1144, a popular rumor claimed that Jews had kidnapped and sacrificed little William of Norwich, and by 1150 the fantasy was generally believed. More than 25 Jews were burned in London in 1189 on the eve of the Third Crusade, and at York in 1190, almost the entire Jewish community was annihilated. The case of "Little Saint Hugh of Lincoln" in 1235, similar to that of William of Norwich, led to the hanging of 19 Jews. By 1200, the stereotype included well poisoning, kidnapping, ritual sacrifice, cannibalism, desecration of the Eucharist, spreading disease, and Devil worship. Such stereotypes have been used against marginal minorities from antiquity to the present and are psychological projections. Christian emphasis upon the physicality of Christ was growing strongly in this period, and the new feast of Corpus Christi (Body of Christ), referring to the true nature of the consecrated Eucharistic host as the real body of Jesus—a feast that grew in popularity in the fourteenth century—is a sign of the increasing veneration of the Eucharist. More than ever, Jews were accused of showing their contempt for Christianity by attacking the Eucharist, and this was perceived as a direct attack upon the person of Christ.

By the end of the century, irrationalism on the subject reached the point that Christians came to believe that the Jews really did realize that the Host was Christ and stole and tortured it in honor of Satan. This fantasy led to fearful massacres of the Jews in 1298. This was a turning point, after which Jews were linked with Satanic witchcraft, dreaded as the willful and knowing agents of the Devil in his attempt to destroy the body of Christ both literally and metaphorically. After 1298, the restraints against antisemitism became increasingly weaker, leading to the appalling massacres between 1348 and 1350, when Jews were accused of being Satan's agents in spreading the Black Death.

Popular rage against the Jews in turn gave rulers such as Philip IV of France (1285–1314) and Edward I of England (1272–1307) an excuse to banish them and confiscate their property. In many areas of Europe, Jews were forced to wear conspicuous colored badges of identification.

The eleventh and twelfth centuries were a period of rapid urban, commercial, and educational growth, producing social tensions that generated varieties of dissent. As regional economic growth picked up and cities strove to achieve political autonomy, heavily traveled trade routes between economic regions developed.

This concatenation spread reformist, political, social, apostolic, and intellectual dissent. Prosecution and persecution of heretics and Jews increased dramatically. Underlying all was the implicit question of distinguishing order from dissent. In the next period the tension was complicated by the addition of a strikingly new kind of heresy in the West: radical dualism.

4

Intellectual and Dualist Heresies: 1140–1184

The midtwelfth century was the most important period in the development of medieval dissent. On the side of order, canon lawyers followed Gratian's *Decretum* in summarizing church law, codifying it, analyzing it logically, and adding to its structure; theologians did the same with church doctrine. The tensions inherent in the conflict between Abelard and Bernard came more closely to the surface. The rise of scholastic thought in the twelfth century, with its set method of dialectic and its desire to define its terms precisely (often in Aristotelian language), forced discussion away from the nonrational, experiential, and aesthetic thought that prevailed earlier and toward highly rational thought. The philosophical Realists who dominated the period believed that human reason illumined by God could establish absolute truths through the use of dialectical reason. They could define ideas as heterodox, outside the bounds of orthodoxy, not only on the old grounds that they were untraditional but on the new grounds that they were irrational. In other words, the fuzzy-bordered nonrational religion of the earlier Middle Ages was transformed by scholastics into *rational theology,* and what they defined out as incorrect was condemned as *irrational* and thus heretical. The political, ecclesiastical forces of order were now powerfully reinforced by both lawyers and theologians, and the lines between orthodoxy and heterodoxy grew steadily firmer.

At the same time, the apostolic movements of the earlier period continued to flourish and expand, with growing emphasis on the doctrine of voluntary poverty. As the wealth and power of the mercantile classes of the growing new cities expanded, and as they and the feudal nobility continued to enrich the churches and monasteries, the outcry against the contrast between the actual daily life of Christians and the ideal, apostolic life became sharper. Protests came from the underprivileged poor, but more eloquently and persuasively from well-to-do literate clergy and laity. The reform movements gathered strength, and the zeal of some reformers exceeded what the orthodox were willing to tolerate.

Some extreme reformists, such as the Humiliati, a twelfth-century group in urban northern Italy that insisted on living the apostolic life of poverty and chastity, rejecting oaths, litigation, wealth, and property, were on the borderline of dissent and orthodoxy. The Humiliati eventually came to follow the orthodox Benedictine Rule and to figure among the strongest preachers against the heretical Cathars. Such zeal, however, frequently crossed over into reformist heresy, especially in the urbanized and industrialized areas of western Germany, northern Italy, the Low Countries, and southern France. Particularly affected were the numerous and relatively well-paid weavers. It was a period of rising expectations for both the urban commercial and artisan classes, and rising expectations provoked dissatisfaction that naturally expressed itself in religious as well as political discourse.

Waldensianism

The strongest and most enduring Reformist heresy of the Middle Ages was founded by Valdes, an influential and wealthy merchant of Lyon. In 1173, Valdes heard the legend of the fifth-century Saint Alexis of Rome, who left his family to live a life of celibacy, and Valdes connected the tale with the parable of the rich young man in Matthew 19: 16–22. Valdes underwent a conversion experience, deciding that his comfortable way of life was incompatible with the Gospels. He provided for his wife, placed his two daughters in the monastery of Fontévraud founded by Robert of Arbrissel, gave the rest of his wealth to the poor, and went out to preach. Belief in the apostolic life had always implied a return to the ideals of the New Testament, but prior to Valdes Reformist leaders were either clergy educated to read Scripture in Latin or else simpler people who were content with what they heard. With spreading literacy, the idea was growing that the text itself was important. Valdes, who knew little Latin, was concerned that the Scripture be translated so that it could be directly learned and directly preached to the people. Under his leadership, the Gospels, other portions of the Bible, and excerpts from the church fathers were translated into French and used as texts for preaching. This circumvented the clergy's claim to be the custodians of the Bible in its authoritative Latin version (the Vulgate of Jerome). It gave dissenters both a more solid base on which to construct their own knowledge and a firmer platform from which to preach to illiterate followers.

Valdes was an eloquent man, persuasive, dynamic, and charismatic, and by 1176 he had attracted a group of followers who were soon preaching to wide audiences in and around Lyon. This directly threatened the authority of the clergy; the archbishop, citing canon law, which forbade preaching without a license, ordered an end to this irregularity. In 1179, Valdes and some of his companions went to Rome to appeal to Pope Alexander III, who was in the midst of the Third Lateran Council, but pope and prelates received them coolly. The pope approved the life of poverty practiced by the Waldensians (Valdes's followers) but refused to interfere with the archbishop's ban on their preaching unless they obtained a license to preach.

Valdes had till now been confident that the authorities would smile on his work; he trusted their own zeal for reform. The authorities were indeed eager for reform, understanding that the growth in dissent proceeded from grave failings in their own moral order and conduct, but they were determined to keep reform under the control of order. It was the perennial problem: with too much order the system becomes sclerotic; with too much dissent it crumbles. Had the archbishop of Lyon been open enough to understand how the Waldensians could have been an energetic force on his side, he could have granted them licenses to preach after undergoing some sort of instruction. But he was as unreceptive to them as before. This caution was not merely a result of the bishops' desire to preserve their own privileges. They had much better reason to fear unlicensed preaching of unapproved doctrines than their predecessors a generation earlier, for in the meantime Catharism, an extreme heresy, was spreading rapidly through Italy, France, and Spain, posing the first organized challenge to the core of orthodox faith since the Germanic people were converted from

Arianism. A true crisis was in the making, and the bishop perhaps feared that the Waldensians would end by joining or supporting the radicals.

Valdes still wished to preach the Scripture without breaking with authority, and in 1180 he agreed to a profession of faith that was essentially an entirely orthodox creed; he specifically rejected Cathar teachings while containing a statement of his own program of voluntary poverty, begging, prohibition of oaths, condemnation of taking human life under any pretext, and exact obedience to the precepts of Christ and the apostles. But the authorities did not respond with a license to preach, and as a result Valdes became bitter and more radical. He now preached justification by internal illumination, the interpretation of the Bible by individuals under the inspiration of the Spirit; the authority of the invisible church—that is, those who are really known to God to be saved, in distinction to the visible, institutional church—and the Apostolic Succession of all the just. Bishops and priests were unneeded, for the faithful could preach, absolve, and consecrate the Eucharist themselves.

Valdes, having been excommunicated in 1182 by Jean de Belles-Mains, archbishop of Lyon, died in obscurity c. 1205. He seems to have lost control of his followers, who became more and more radical and, like Francis of Assisi later, he seems to have withdrawn from the effort to keep his followers to his original teachings. The Waldensians split into a number of groups, some more radical than others. Among Waldensian teachings were that husbands and wives ought to separate and live in chastity (probably showing Cathar influence). Although their leaders eventually became a sort of clergy, they denied the necessity of a sacrificing priesthood, arguing that every just man or woman held the sacramental power of consecrating the Eucharist and of forgiving sins. They did so in the belief that leading a holy life rather than holding ecclesiastical office imparts authority. They wandered the countryside and the towns preaching in the vernacular and encouraging the literate to read the Bible and the illiterate to memorize biblical passages.

Women and men alike held leadership roles among the Waldensians. Owing to the support of women, to widespread preaching and teaching, and to the fact that the Waldensians were the heirs to all previous Reformist heresy, their influence was so wide and persistent that they have survived persecution, the Protestant

Reformation, and secularism to continue even today. An indication of the fluidity of the boundaries between dissent and order is that both the Waldensians and the Humiliati defended orthodoxy against the dualist Cathars. While popes regarded them as outside the boundaries of orthodoxy, they considered themselves among the orthodox while excluding and condemning more radical dissenters.

The new reformist insistence upon both the Bible and personal illumination, as opposed to either scholastic reason or episcopal tradition, indicates the degree to which the organized church was threatened. The Humiliati and the Waldensians, along with Arnold-ists (followers of Arnold of Brescia) and Patarenes (by now like *publicans* a generalized term for all Reformist heretics) were con-demned in the decree *Ad abolendam* issued by Pope Lucius III at the Council of Verona in 1184 with the backing of the Emperor Frederick I.

Ad abolendam was the first clear definition of heresy as a legal offense. This decree had roots in Gratian's 1140 *Decretum*, which gave temporal as well as spiritual authorities responsibility for the prosecution of heresy. The direct precedents for the decree were the Treaty of Venice (1177), in which Pope Hadrian IV and the Emperor Frederick I agreed to harness church and state together against heresy; legislation against heresy at Toulouse in 1178; and the Third Lateran Council (1179). This council issued definitions of heresy, orders for the excommunication of heretics, and rewards for those who struggled against them. But Verona was the first explicit general condemnation of heresy in Christendom by both temporal and spiritual authorities since the Theodosian Code. It deliberately and explicitly brought the secular and temporal powers together as joint defenders of orthodoxy. It became the model for the crushing prohibition of heresy issued by the Fourth Lateran Council under Innocent III in 1215.

After 1184, repression of the Waldensians in southern France tended to move them into Lombardy, a more receptive area for heterodoxy, and into the Alps. Lombardy, home of Arnold of Brescia and of the Patarenes, produced yet another heresy, that of the Speronisti, followers of Ugo Speroni. Speroni, a lawyer, began a movement in the late 1170s that took a more anticlerical position than even the Waldensians. Speroni denied the priesthood, not simply on the basis that it had become corrupt, but on the grounds that there was no scriptural basis for it. The sacraments could be ignored as inventions of the clergy. The internal illumination of the Holy Spirit was all the baptism the Speronisti needed. The growing importance of the Bible in the dissenting textual communities was the core of the third great challenge to traditional episcopal order. All of these challenges set other sources of authority—internal illumination, rational deduction, and now the biblical text, against the order of Apostolic Succession.

Dualist Heresy

A more radical threat to orthodox order than any Reformist dissent was the new heresy imported in the 1140s from Bulgaria and Illyria: Bogomilism. The reasons for the arrival of the Bogomil missionaries in the 1140s and their success are not yet fully understood. Prosecutions of Bogomils in the Balkans or unsettled economic situations there may have caused them to move westward. Western reception of Bogomilism built upon previous contacts with eastern dualism through trade and crusade and even more upon the existing Reformist heresies. This reception created a new Western heresy, Catharism. The Cathars converted many Reformist heretics and extended their influence through wide areas of Italy, France, and Spain. Although some of the Reformists were co–opted, others opposed the Cathars as too radical. For Catharism was far more than a Reformist doctrine; it was the revival of a radical dualism that Christian tradition had rejected for a thousand years.

The Cathars preached a strict dualism between spirit and matter, including, among the more extreme, a belief in two gods, one lord of spirit and the other of matter, the latter being equated with the Devil. This kind of doctrine could in no way be accommodated within traditional Christianity; it had already been debated with the Gnostics in the first two centuries and the Manicheans in the following two and discarded. Dualism, however, had always been able to find a foothold in Christianity for the simple reason that Christianity always had a degree of inherent tendency in that direction. Influenced by Platonism, Christianity early distinguished between spirit and matter, soul and body, taking matter and body as inferior. Early Christianity drew from Apocalyptic Judaism the tendency to shift the blame for evil from God to the Devil. Although orthodox Christianity always insisted that Satan was a creature inferior to God, the Gnostics tended to see God and Satan as opposite spiritual powers. Further, the Gnostics perceived the Devil as the lord or even the creator of matter and the body. Christianity repudiated such views yet was influenced by them. Christianity considered Satan enormously powerful and mistrusted matter and the body as his domain.

So Christian theology already had moderate dualistic tendencies, and the emphasis on asceticism shared by reforming monks and theologians with Reformist heretics further encouraged these tendencies. When the Cathars appeared in Italy in the 1140s, in the midst of the radical reform movement, they shared with the Reformist heretics their contempt for corrupt clergy. Some of the reformists were therefore prepared to receive the Bogomil missionaries with enthusiasm. Others, more wary, joined the Catholics in firmly rejecting the Bogomils.

The tension and split among the reformist heretics with the advent of Catharism is revealed in two documents about heresy at Cologne: a letter of Everwin (a prior of the Premonstratensian house of Steinfeld) to Bernard of Clairvaux in 1143, and a book of 13 sermons by Ekbert of Schönau written 20 years later, about 1163. Everwin sent Bernard a description of a sect of heretics that he had observed in Cologne. Their doctrines were typically Reformist, emphasizing the unworthiness of the corrupt clergy, denying the sacraments (except baptism) and affirming internal illumination, which made fasting and penance unnecessary. They held that any belief or practice not explicitly sanctioned by the New Testament was invalid and that there was no Scriptural mandate for Apostolic Succession or an ordained priesthood. Some of the heretics, however, held views that betokened an alien influence: they rejected marriage and refused to eat meat, dairy products, or eggs— anything connected with reproduction. They distinguished between auditors, believers, and elect—a mark of the Cathars—and they claimed that their ideas were ancient and came from the East.

Curiously, many of the orthodox opponents of Catharism agreed that the sect was ancient, identifying it with the Manicheism that Augustine and other fathers had struggled against in the fourth century. They did this because they assumed that all heresies are essentially the same, originating with Satan. But despite similarities, the Cathars were not Manicheans. For one thing, doctrines and practices had changed and developed from ancient times through Armenia, Bulgaria, and Illyria; for another, Catharism was never monolithic, and from the 1170s it was badly split between the moderate and the extreme wings.

The Cathars had clever ways of introducing their doctrines into Reformist circles; they would begin with the usual sort of Reformist ideas and then, having "softened people up," gradually introduce them to the real, secret teachings of their religion.

By the time Ekbert of Schönau, who with his sister Elizabeth and Hildegard of Bingen mounted a formidable Benedictine homiletic campaign against heretics in the Rhineland, wrote his sermon *Adversus catharos* (*Against the Cathars*), in 1163, the Cologne heretics were no longer divided, for the old-fashioned Reformists had been dominated and absorbed by the Cathars. The group now held typical Cathar views, including reincarnation and the initiation of converts by the laying on of hands; they were led by "perfects"; instead of Christian feasts, they celebrated their own. They used the *consolamentum,* the laying on of hands, instead of baptism for the remission of sins. They affirmed that all matter and all flesh were created by Satan, and that Christ did not have a real body and was not born of the Virgin Mary.

The Cathars spread rapidly in the Rhineland and may have influenced the heretics condemned in England from 1163 to 1166. These isolated heretics were less a sign of growth of heresy in England (never significant before the fourteenth century) than a sign of King Henry II's stern measures to construct and enforce both temporal and spiritual order in his realm. His strict legislation, in other words, made heretics of those who previously might have been considered dissenters or simply marginal.

The Cathars were most powerful in southern France, northern Italy, and Catalonia. Unlike the Waldensians or other earlier medieval heretics, the Cathars consciously and deliberately thought of themselves as *not* being Catholics: they represented a true church, a true tradition, Catharism, which was in substance and tradition completely separate from Catholicism and represented the true teachings of Christ. The fact that the Cathars exaggerated their actual historical separation from orthodoxy does not remove the sociologically significant fact that they believed themselves to be an independent church. But some modern historians, mistakenly accepting their rhetoric, viewed Catharism as a separate religion rather than as a Christian heresy.

From the 1140s into the 1160s, the dominant form of Catharism was mitigated (more moderate); these Cathars (sometimes called

Concorezzenses or Garatenses) affirmed God's lordship over Satan. In the 1160s a more extreme view, absolute dualism, was introduced by "Papa Nicetas," a missionary from Illyria. Nicetas arrived in Lombardy about 1166, denying that the consolamentum of the mitigated, Western Cathars, was valid. Lombardy, like southern France, was fertile ground because of the existence of so many heretics in the region already, owing to its advanced commercial economy. Nicetas's followers were called the order of Dragovitsa (later also called Drugonthia or Desenzano.) Most of the Lombard Cathars accepted the new, absolute teaching and received a new *consolamentum* (were "reconsoled") by Nicetas, who also reorganized their hierarchy. Although the Cathars of France and Aragon resisted absolute dualism, it gradually spread into the Midi, until by the end of the century radicals dominated almost everywhere. The essential belief of the absolute Cathars was that there were two gods, the Lord and the Devil, locked in eternal cosmic conflict.

The Cathars, although splitting into an increasing diversity of sects, were so powerful in the Midi that they were able to hold open debates at Lombers (1165) and at St.-Félix de Caraman (1167). They attracted large numbers of followers from among reformist heretics, from some orthodox clergy, from the townspeople, and even from the nobility. Their influence lasted well into the thirteenth century.

Cathar teaching and practice varied in time and place, but the variety of sources permits a description of its fundamental teachings and practices. Two opposing forces operate in the world: one spiritual and good, the other evil and devoted to corrupting spirit by matter. Whether ultimately dependent upon God or whether an independent deity himself, the evil spirit created the material world in order to entrap spirits. Because the Old Testament refers to God as creator of the world, the God of the Old Testament must be Satan (a doctrine that incidentally abetted antisemitism), and the Old Testament itself must be rejected wholly or at least in part. Human beings' souls are spiritual and therefore good; bodies are evil; we must strive to liberate our spirit from our flesh. We may do this only by becoming Cathars; otherwise the soul will be condemned at death to be reincarnated in yet another corrupt body.

Water being corrupt matter, baptism was replaced by the *consolamentum* as the initiatory rite. The *consolamentum* was the central sacrament of Catharism whose outward and visible sign was a perfect's laying of hands on a believer. Christ was the divine messenger, the greatest angel, of the spiritual, hidden God. Christ did not have a material body; he only took the appearance of one in order to communicate his message to us: the message that we must free our souls from our bodies. Christ therefore did not really suffer on the cross, die, or rise from the dead; he saved us not by dying for us but by conveying the "message." Because all matter was evil, the Eucharist was an imposture, and any material object, whether icon, relic, or cross, should be shunned if not destroyed.

The orthodox, Catholic church was an institution conceived by the Devil to keep humans enslaved to the lie. In place of the orthodox hierarchy, the Cathars had bishops of their own, a fact intensely irritating to orthodox order. The Cathars are one of the clearest examples of heretical groups organizing themselves to create an ecclesiastical structure in competition with the Catholic church. Each Cathar bishop had two elected assistant bishops and a deacon; the associate bishops had the right of succession when the old bishop died. Local Cathars were organized into groups in which a division was sharply drawn between the *perfecti* (the perfect) and the *credentes* (the believers). Although no formal ritual probably was necessary to become a believer, believers were required to make the *melioramentum*, a formal reverence, upon encountering a perfect. To perform the *melioramentum*, the believer genuflected three times and begged the perfect to pray that he or she too might attain perfection. The believers were under the authority of the perfects.

If a believer wished to become a perfect, he or she took the *consolamentum*. A probationary period of at least a year was required, during which the believer had to behave like a perfect in fasting, avoiding meat and other food associated with coition (such as meat and eggs), and completely abstaining from sex, before he or she could receive the *consolamentum*. Because reception of the *consolamentum* erased all one's previous sins, most Cathars put it off until dying. This made the perfects who received it earlier in life a small elite. In certain areas, the *endura*, fasting unto death, was occasionally administered to children or the ill, with the express purpose of effecting the speedy liberation of the soul. In these instances the *consolamentum* was administered toward the end of the ordeal; if one happened to survive, one became a perfect.

The perfect wore special black clothing and was expected to lead a life of utter purity, because the *consolamentum* could not be repeated; to sin after receiving it was to be condemned to reincarnation. (Some Cathar groups allowed a private "reconsolation" for sinners.) The Cathars did not believe in hell or damnation: either one was redeemed by accepting the message and receiving the consolamentum, or one was sent back into another body—human or animal—for another life of suffering and testing.

The Cathars practiced three long fasts annually. Once a month they held a service at which petty errors were confessed and forgiven. An elaborate ritual feast, the Bema, was practiced annually. The *perfecti* lived lives of ascetic rigor. They forbade oaths; they rejected luxury and wealth (at least in theory; Cathar nobles did not readily give up their castles). They abstained from meat, partly because of their belief in reincarnation, partly because of their disgust for flesh and for procreation. Belief in reincarnation also prohibited them from killing most animals: the pig in question might be your uncle. Marriage and all heterosexual intercourse was condemned, for the worst possible act was to conceive a child, thereby entrapping another soul in a loathsome body. The aversion to procreation may have permitted sexual acts that could not lead to conception: perhaps for this reason, the Cathars were said to be homosexual, and the modern slang *bugger* comes from French *bougre*, derived from Bulgaria, the home of the Bogomils. But the "believers" were not under the same compulsion to sinlessness as the "perfect," and *credentes* frequently had intercourse—and children.

The strength of Catharism, its rapid spread, and the fact that it could be extirpated only by force, derives from several sources. One was the influence of women. Men and women were equal in Catharism (except that women could not be bishops), and male believers were subject to female perfects. Catholic women could not be priests or professors, and they could obtain positions of authority only in female monasteries. Furthermore, membership in such institutions was being restricted, only by dowry requirements, to the wealthy. Much less often literate than men, women became bearers of an oral tradition that could be enormously influential. Historians have naturally always downplayed the spoken as opposed to the written word, having little access to the former, so it is likely that women had much more influence than has been assumed, both among the orthodox and the heretics. Orthodox laywomen could enter beguinages (monastic houses for laypeople) in Flanders and northern France—indeed, more than 30 beguinages still exist today in northern Europe—but beguinages did not exist in the south. On the other hand, numerous houses for women perfects were established in the Midi, allowing Cathar women a ready path to independence and even power. Furthermore, in southern France, which was under Roman law, women could legally transfer property to the Cathar churches. The advantage Cathar women held over Catholic women was slight, but in the Midi enough to have an influence. The appeal of Catharism was strongly regional, capitalizing upon the cultural hostility of the Midi toward the north. It also cut sharply across class lines, attracting nobles, merchants, and artisans of both sexes.

The Cathars were the most radical threat to Christian orthodoxy in centuries, and the agents of order felt obliged to repress them or face disintegration. Order became more effective in the pursuit of heresy during the twelfth century as canon law, parish organization, and episcopal visitations were established. A shift in the theological perception of heresy also took place. Previously, the agents of order had been concerned with public dissent that openly challenged order. Now, as fear of heresy grew along with the means of combating it, they investigated private views as well.

"The Inquisition"

The ecclesiastical establishment maintained some of the practices—or at least terminologies—of Roman law, including *inquisitio*. An *inquisitio* was a legal investigation of a question used in both civil and religious administration. For example, William the Conqueror's census known as Domesday Book (1087) was an *inquisitio*. In medieval canon law, *inquisitio* simply meant the bishops' duty to investigate the problems of their dioceses. This was already clear in Regino of Prüm's tenth-century collection of canons, which specifically included the duty of the bishop to visit parts of his diocese annually.

There was never such an entity as "The Inquisition." Two common misperceptions must be obliterated. The first is that a centralized institution in the Middle Ages called "The Inquisition," an organization aimed at suppressing dissent, ever existed; in fact, such an institution is pure fantasy. Prosecutions of heretics did exist, conducted by a variety of authorities, especially bishops and princes. And certain ecclesiastics—Bernard Gui in the fourteenth century for example—were given special commissions as "inquisitors." But "there was never a permanently constituted congregation and tribunal against heresy until the sixteenth century."[9] Second, inquisitions were by no means restricted to, or even focused on, investigation or prosecution of dissent.

To the contrary, inquisitions or investigations were concerned with individual sins and crimes and as such were carried out by both the civil and clerical authorities. English criminal law was largely inquisitorial, with judges conducting investigations into the validity of criminal charges. The functions sometimes melded, for heretics were often also accused of immorality. The inquisitions tended to focus on heresies more than on sins because heresies were usually more corporate, visible, and easily prosecutable. The most famous inquisition, the Spanish Inquisition, did not begin until 1478 and became a department of state in 1483.

The fallacy of "The Inquisition" formed part of a closely woven pattern of fallacy about ignorant flat-earth medievals, repressive popes, evil Spaniards—in short, the fallacy of the Dark Ages. Although the components are all false or at best grossly exaggerated, they reinforced each other in a way that provided an empirically false view of the world that has distorted historical writing.

What actually happened is that a particular variety of inquisition evolved, along with other inquisitions, in the twelfth century: inquiry into people's religious beliefs or practices. Investigations into heresy became common only from the Third Lateran Council in 1179, which condemned the Waldensians and other reform heretics, under the influence of Henry of Marcy, Abbot of Clairvaux, who had been preaching in southern France and encountered the heretics face to face. The council authorized Henry to use force against heresy, and in 1181 he launched a small military attack on the heretics, prefiguring the vast military movements of the Albigensian Crusade later. The Third Lateran Council put a seal on the efforts of the Reform papacy and the canon lawyers to define theology and law. The period from 1140 to 1184 was crucial in two ways: first in the rise of two of the most important heretical movements in the Middle Ages—the Cathars and Waldensians—and second in the beginning of formal investigations of heresy.

5

Spiritual and Apocalyptic Heresies: 1184–1250

Order's Counterattack

The eleventh and early twelfth centuries had been a time when dissent increased more swiftly than measures against it. The decree *Ad abolendam* (1184) was the first stern muster of order's counterattack, which under Innocent III (1198–1216) turned the balance. Whereas charity and persuasion had hitherto been the favored way of dealing with dissent, coercion now became the rule. During the thirteenth century, dissent continued, but order used persuasion, law, and sheer force to suppress it. The strategy was to attack the dissenters on all fronts.

Debates were held and treatises written to persuade the educated away from heresy. Professors took little part at first. Most thirteenth-century theologians such as William of Auvergne or William of Auxerre paid heresy little heed. Usually attacks on heresy came from the pens of polemicists or the exhortations of preachers. Preachers, including converted heretics, were licensed and sent forth, and orders of friars founded, to convert heretics. A new requirement that communion and private confession be made at least once annually was intended as a means of inculcating or ensuring correct doctrinal beliefs. Condemnations by popes, secular authorities, and councils along the lines of Verona were issued. The revival of Roman law and the growth of centralized political power and codes of civil law brought the secular arm into the repression of dissent again to a degree unheard of since the late Roman Empire. Laws were formalized that defined dissent as heresy and criminalized those who helped heretics. Crusades were preached, fought, and won, and ever stricter inquisitorial processes managed to root out and destroy most dissent. Punishment for persistent heresy included excommunication (exclusion from the sacraments and isolation from the community), expulsion (banishment), flogging, branding, prison, death and confiscation of property, and even exhumation and burning of the deceased. Burning was of course symbolic of purification, but it also had the effect of removing any relics that sectaries might have saved and venerated. Steps were taken to demoralize heretics by isolating them socially. The extremes were death or incarceration, of course, but banishment or expulsion were often deadly in a society as communitarian as medieval cities or countryside. Even at the mildest end of the spectrum, labeling a person as a heretic to be shunned separated him or her from the community and was a powerful inducement to recant.

A subtler, perhaps almost unconscious, strategy of the papacy against the heretics was rhetorical. As many of the heretics claimed authority directly from Christ, Innocent III shifted the traditional papal title, vicar of Peter, to vicar of Christ, thereby asserting a direct link to the sole source of all legitimate authority.

The influence of the Waldensians waned, partly because of investigations but mainly because of schisms within their own ranks. In 1205, Valdes and his faithful followers the Lyonists split with a larger group, the Poor Lombards, under the leadership of John di Paolo. The Lyonists continued to preach a moderate Reformist heterodoxy, but the Lombards became more radically anticlerical. In 1218, representatives of the two groups met near Bergamo but failed to find grounds for reunion. Some of the Lyonists joined the Lombards, some returned to the Catholic church, and some remained faithful to the teachings of Valdes. The Waldensians were spared the destruction suffered by the Cathars precisely because they were considered far less dangerous, but in the Rhineland the papal investigator Conrad of Marburg pursued them vigorously until his assassination in 1233.

Among the first of the successful debaters and polemicists against heresy was Durand of Huesca, a former Waldensian converted to orthodoxy during a debate at Pamiers in southern France in 1207. He had preached effectively against the Cathars as a Waldensian and had written the *Liber antihaeresis, Antiheretical Book,* against them in 1191–92. Now he was licensed to continue to combat the Cathars as a Catholic.

The Order of Preachers (Dominicans), founded by Dominic in 1216, had from its beginning the explicit purpose of preaching to all the laity and above all to heretics and pagans. The Dominicans became the leading preachers against heresy in southern France, and later they were effective inquisitors. Innocent III used the Franciscan Order for much the same purpose.

Nowhere was the linking of spirituality with heresy more ironic than in the development of the Franciscan Order. Francis of Assisi (1182–1226) was the son of a rich merchant; in his youth he pursued worldly ambitions. After being held as a prisoner of war and suffering a long illness, he decided to live his life in imitation of Christ, especially Christ's poverty. Francis's success in this endeavor led to his veneration through the ages, even to the point of being called *alter Christus,* another Christ. For Francis, both external poverty (renunciation of wealth) and internal poverty (renunciation of pride and ambition) were necessary. He soon attracted followers, and this produced an impossible quandary. Practically speaking, apostolic poverty cannot serve as a basis for the life of a community, so the group's efforts to imitate Christ fully necessarily failed after Francis had attracted more than a few followers. Francis realized that for large numbers a rule was necessary, and the first Franciscan rule was established in 1209. Aware that previous preachers of apostolic poverty such as Valdes had been condemned, Francis and his followers sought and obtained approval from Innocent. Thus Francis submitted to ecclesiastical order and was glad of its support. But it was impossible to transfer the charisma of the inspired Francis to a large religious order. Francis had been prophetic, marginal, whereas the Franciscans soon became a part of ecclesiastical order. The Franciscan Order wandered far from its founder's own vision, which was that through poverty, prayer, and charitable action, the soul could approach God and through its example draw others with it. Even before Francis's death, the leaders of the order diluted his vision, and Francis withdrew from active participation in the order into almost a hermit's life at La Verna, where he died in 1226.

The idea of official crusades against infidels went back as far as the seventh century, but it was effectively revived by Pope Urban II when he preached the First Crusade against the Muslims in 1096. The twelfth century saw the Second and Third Crusades. The disastrous Fourth Crusade of 1204, when the might of the Latin Church was diverted against the Greek Church and the Greek Empire, provoked divisions and hatreds that still persist. Given the failure of the eastern crusades, the notion of pursuing crusades against enemies in western Europe itself readily occurred. The Cathars were the chosen target.

At the beginning of the thirteenth century, the papacy, implicitly admitting that preaching and persuasion were failing, and recognizing that Catharism had gained extensive political support among the higher nobility of southern France and Aragon, was ready to take organized military action. The assassination of the papal legate Pierre de Castelnau in 1208 provided the cause for war. Count Raymond VI of Toulouse, whom Pierre had previously excommunicated, was implicated. Innocent III, although in principle opposed to the death penalty for heretics, genuinely feared that the Cathars posed a threat to the survival of the Catholic church. He proclaimed an official crusade, which was avidly supported by the northern French nobility, who saw in it the opportunity to acquire valuable land in the south by conquest and confiscation. After the 1208 crusade was launched, Raymond VI and his son Raymond VII, with their rich and extensive lands, were among the military leaders of the resistance against the crusaders. Under the ecclesiastical leadership of Arnold Amalric, Archbishop of Narbonne, and the political and military leadership of Simon de Montfort, the Albigensian Crusade, named after the Cathar stronghold at Albi in southern France, was pursued ruthlessly. The crusaders won a major battle at Muret in 1213 and gradually emerged victorious over the Albigensian forces. By 1229, the crusade was over and the Albigensian strongholds eliminated. Large sections of the population still held to the heresy, however, and a century of investigation and force was needed to eliminate it, the bloodiest moment being the massacre of Cathars at Montségur in 1244. Inquisitorial prosecution of Cathars continued in the early fourteenth century.

The Albigensian Crusade was unique, explainable in terms of a perceived enormous political and religious threat posed by the Cathars to all of Christian society. Crusades could be effective only where dissent enjoyed focused political and military support. It was too expensive, cumbersome, and inefficient to deal with small numbers of localized dissenters. The further development of official investigations was a much more effective weapon. Here again, the Council of Verona was the standard.

Ad abolendam became the pattern for episcopal investigations into heresy. The *inquisitio heretice pravitatis* (investigation of heresy) was only one of many types of inquisition, but it is the one that affected the tension between dissent and order. The decree defined a number of heresies, including Catharism and Waldensianism. It implicitly distinguished between unwitting heterodoxy and genuine heresy by defining heretics as those who after warning persisted in defying legitimate authority. Heretical clergymen were to be defrocked and turned over to the secular courts, as were heretical laypeople. *Ad abolendam* mandated that bishops make tours of parishes twice a year when any indication of heresy was found in the region. The decree made clear, as did the Albigensian Crusade, that the struggle against heresy was no longer primarily theological; rather, it was a concentrated effort by the leaders of ecclesiastical and civil order to preserve and enhance their powers at a time when those powers were perceived to be under serious attack.

Innocent III's measures against heretics included not only encouraging new preaching orders and the Albigensian Crusade but also new legislation. In 1199, the new pope issued a decree aimed at heretics in Viterbo, *Vergentis in senium*, which explicitly assimilated the religious crime of heresy to the old Roman *crimen laesae majestatis*, the crime of treason. *Vergentis* ordered the expulsion of heretics from the city, and it became a precedent widely adopted in collections of legal canons. In a Christian society where the secular and the spiritual powers worked together as one, heretics were traitors. They now incurred all the punishments of treason under Roman law, including the death penalty and confiscation of all property except the heretic's house, which was to be burnt to the ground. The idea was that the spiritual authorities would pronounce on the guilt of a heretic and that the secular authorities would administer the punishments. This idea was explicitly stated in Innocent's 1207 decree, *Cum ex officii nostri*. A person judged a heretic by an ecclesiastical court was to be handed over to the secular authorities for *animadversione debita*, a crucial term that is difficult to translate. Literally meaning "for due attention," it involved both the act of turning the convicted heretic over to secular judicial cognizance, and also the full implication that the secular court would impose the appropriate penalty, usually death.

The canons issued by Innocent III's Fourth Lateran Council dealt with virtually every major problem confronting Christian society at that point, but the very first canons condemned heresies, refining the procedures set forth at Verona. The decretal *Qualiter et quando* of the council established the *inquisitio ex officio* as the standard method of trial in all ecclesiastical courts from rural archdeacons to popes. The *inquisitio heretice pravitatis* was only one kind of inquisition, and investigators into heresy had no special powers that other investigators lacked. Still, they had one powerful moral weapon. Where earlier dissenters could justify their resistance to authority by often valid claims that the authorities condemning them were immoral, such a defense was less easy to make with the inquisitors, who were usually as honest and ascetic as they were unyielding. Innocent's successors Honorius III (1216–27), Gregory IX (1227–41), and Innocent IV (1243–54) continued the prosecution of heretics.

As towns grew larger and as civil and ecclesiastical authorities more firmly controlled the countryside, the old sense of community declined. As prosecution of heresy became more intense, people were afraid not to bear witness against friends or neighbors for fear of being declared heretics or at least *fautores* (helpers) of heretics themselves. Finally, individuals might profit from the confiscation of a heretic's property.

The fact that even the Albigensian Crusade did not entirely extirpate the Cathars led both temporal and spiritual order to establish permanent laws. In Germany, the law code *Sachsenspiegel* (1230) decreed secular punishment for heresy, as did the law *Cupientes* (1229) of Louis IX of France, which ordered royal officials to investigate reports of heresy and bring heretics to justice. Temporal and spiritual rulers worked together to preserve order against dissent. The more firmly societal order was defined, the more dissenters were defined as heretics.

The social corollary of these religious and secular measures was a growing marginalization of certain groups of people, their exclusion from the pattern of Christian society. Thirteenth-century ecclesiastical rhetoric also returned to the ancient idea that heretics were the army of Satan against Christian society. Bernard of Clairvaux had already used strong language against the heretics, calling Henry of Lausanne a "hungry wolf" and heretics in general obstacles set by Satan in the path of the church. In the thirteenth century, increasing fear of heresy led to the concept of "infected" areas and of heresy as a disease: terms such as *leprosy, plague,* and *deadly fever* were increasingly applied to heresies and heretics. Such cancers had to be cut out of the body of Christendom and destroyed lest they infect others and eventually destroy the church.

Such terminology was a rhetorical strategy against heretics, but it was not empty verbiage. Although in reality heresy did not exist as a monolithic entity, but varied greatly in time and place, by the twelfth century the orthodox were beginning to believe that it actually was a monolithic threat. The source of all heresy was Satan; its purpose to block the Kingdom of God. Heresy was an absolute evil, and heretics were readily linked with Jews, pagans, magicians, Muslims, and other "Antichrists" in a conspiracy against Christ and his community the orthodox church. Thus, "heresy" attained a special reality in the minds of the orthodox, a matter of great significance, because people act on what they believe to be true rather than what may actually be true.

Canon law became more powerful as well as more precise: Innocent III, Gregory IX, and Innocent IV were all trained canonists. Canon law was the permanent underpinning of the struggle of order against dissent. The canon lawyers' definitions of a heretic included any of the following: one who perverts the sacraments; one who deliberately isolates himself from the Christian community; one who errs in interpreting Scripture; one who founds a new sect; one who believes differently about the articles of faith than the Roman church does; one who publicly and persistently teaches error.

These theoretical definitions were expanded in the actual practice of the prosecution: for example, by the thirteenth century, inquisitors were already diligently inquiring into people's private beliefs even when they kept public silence. Individual motivation was not a concern of the agents of order. It no more occurred to them that a heretic could be thoughtful, prayerful, and sincere in his or her beliefs than it would have occurred to American political authorities in the mid–twentieth century that there could be honest, thoughtful Communists. All Communists were servants of the Kremlin just as all heretics were servants of Satan.

In the first year of his reign, Gregory IX published an encyclical letter to the cities of Lombardy demanding their closer cooperation in the repression of heresy. He followed this with a severe decree, *Ille humani generis* (1231), imitating the Fourth Lateran Council in specifically characterizing heresies as the work of the Devil. It appointed a papal judge delegate with the responsibility of preaching against heresy and of identifying obdurate heretics who needed prosecution. In the same year, Gregory issued the decretal *Excommunicamus*, specifying that the due punishment appropriate to obdurate heretics was death and confiscation. Gregory sent special investigators to certain badly "infected" areas: Conrad of Marburg to the Rhineland and Robert le Bougre to France. From this time, such agents bore the formal title of "inquisitor."

Increasing papal reliance upon Dominicans and Franciscans with orders from Rome to some extent supplanted investigations of heresy by local bishops. But although numerous papal inquisitions were held, especially in central Italy, which was politically controlled by Rome, there never was a centralized "Papal Inquisition" with control over all of Latin Europe (or even all of Italy). Rather, the pattern of legislation against heresy was a mix of papal, episcopal, and secular laws. The Council of Tarragona in 1242 provided detailed definitions of heretics as those obstinate in error but also condemned the hiders, receivers, defenders, and aiders of heretics. The manual issued for inquisitors at Carcassonne (c. 1248) helped Innocent IV (1243–54) and Alexander IV (1254–61) to proceed to even stricter definitions. Innocent IV's decrees *Ad extirpanda* (1252) and *Ad negotium* (1254) were fierce weapons against heresy. From 1184 to 1250, order prevailed over heresies that order had itself in part created by definition.

Joachim of Fiore

But dissenters created their own heresies as well. The most influential was Joachim of Fiore (1135–1202).[10] Like many Reformist leaders, Joachim came from a wealthy and influential family, and he held an official post at the Sicilian royal court. After a conversion experience to the apostolic life in 1170, he became a monk and then abbot of Corazzo, a Cistercian monastery in Calabria. Joachim was more than a Reformist. In 1183, he began having visions, which he experienced in true prophetic fashion as illuminations from the Holy Spirit. These experiences led him to a new theological perspective, almost a new theological worldview. He argued that intellectual, theological efforts to attain truth were as water that needed to be transformed into wine by the power of the Holy Spirit. He argued implicitly that three sources of authority exist in the church: bishops, theologians, and those inspired by the Holy Spirit. Insisting that he was not a prophet and had no new revelation, Joachim nonetheless claimed a spiritual understanding of Scripture, a deeper, mystical reading than theologians could obtain. He emphasized history more than any Christian writer since Orosius in the fifth century, and not only history but the action of the Holy Trinity in history—God's moving force through time. The underlying idea was that God is gradually bringing the world in stages to fulfillment.

Joachim stood within the broad tradition of apocalyptic thought, whose origins lie in the Jewish–Christian apocalyptic literature of the centuries just before and after Christ, the most famous example of which is the Book of Revelation in the New Testament. Apocalyptic (which literally means "unwrapping" or "unveiling") involves the following: First, prophecy (both in the root sense of "speaking out God's word" and in the secondary sense of speaking God's word about the present and future). Second, eschatology (*eschata*), concern with the last things, the end of the world. Third, the sense that the end of the world is at hand. Many Christian theologians were (and are) eschatological, perceiving God as working through history teleologically, toward an end in time, but without the apocalyptic sense that the end was to be immediate and violent. Fourth, the sense that the end would entail a final battle between good and evil followed by the Second Coming of Christ. Fifth, the sense that the end would terminate space and time and move directly into eternity, with salvation for the chosen just. Specifically, therefore, Christian apocalyptic is hopeful prophecy of the immediate transformation of this world into joyful eternity. Most Christian apocalyptic writing was, if not "mainstream," perfectly orthodox. Some apocalyptic writers were isolated prophets, some rebellious clergy, but most apocalyptic writing from Augustine's time onward came from sophisticated and educated clergy.

Three popes—Lucius III (1181–85), Urban III (1185–87), and Clement III (1187–91)—impressed by Joachim's monastic reforms and above all by his skill at biblical exegesis, encouraged him in his work. But his views grew more radical. At first he envisioned his three ages loosely, but then about 1200 he or one of his followers drew up the *Liber figurarum* (*Book of Patterns,*) with a complex scheme involving "stages," "times," and "ages." At this point Joachism became millenarian, a usually heterodox subset of apocalyptic thought involving the notion of fixed, predetermined "ages."

Joachim's Age of the Father, from Adam to Isaiah, was the time of law, of childish obedience, dominated by married people. The Age of the Son, from Isaiah to the present, is dominated by Christ's redemption of humanity from sin and by the authority of the clergy. The third age, the Age of the Holy Spirit, had been conceived in the time of Saint Benedict of Nursia in the sixth century and was gradually being brought to parturition by the Holy Spirit working through celibate reform monks. This New Age would be preceded by the brief rule of an Antichrist successfully resisted by a holy pope and reformed monks. Then the New Age itself would emerge, characterized by lives of contemplation spent in perfect liberty in Christian love under the guidance of the reformed, spiritual, and illumined monasteries. After this age of earthly perfection would come the second Antichrist, the final battle, and the end of time.[11]

The Joachist scheme emphasized salvation through the visible working of the Holy Spirit in history, which was to be induced by, and would in turn vindicate, the ideals of reform, especially reform monasticism.

After Joachim's death in 1202, his influence spread throughout Europe, dominating all theories about eschatology and fuelling a number of heresies after his death. Large numbers of millenarian writings such as Arnold of Villanova's *The Time of the Coming of the Antichrist* (1297) followed Joachim and elaborated upon his thought. Joachim's thought merged with that of the scholastic Amalric of Bena, who died in 1206. Amalric was condemned posthumously at Paris in 1210 as a pantheist on the basis of his interpretation of John Scottus Eriugena, who had been essentially ignored between the ninth century and the twelfth. (Eriugena's work, having at last been understood, was condemned in 1225 for pantheistic tendencies.)

The Contemptative Tradition

A religious attitude emerging in the twelfth century and symbolized by the work of Joachim and Amalric can, with caution, be called *mysticism*. But both Joachim and Amalric were condemned by the Fourth Lateran Council, a bad omen for the reception of mysticism. The term *mysticism* was not invented until the eighteenth century, so no medieval persons thought of themselves as mystics, and the term is best avoided. In the Middle Ages, the terminology that would have been best understood was the *contemplative tradition.*

The contemplative tradition combines a deep, personal experience, a sense of illumination, a change in one's way of life as a result of the experience, and (sometimes) a sense of union with, or at least close bonding with, God. Contemplation had been present in the early church, especially under the influence of Pseudo-Dionysius in the sixth century, but Pseudo-Dionysius was unknown in the West until he was revived by Eriugena, who was in turn only understood in the twelfth century. From the eleventh and twelfth centuries, an indigenous Western comtemplative tradition arose, flowing from monastic reform and especially from the Cistercian Order. As long as contemplative spirituality was connected with established monastic communities, which could keep it orthodox while drawing nourishment from it, the forces of order viewed it as a positive force. Later, some individual contemplatives would hold views condemned as heretical.

With the re-creation of a more sophisticated philosophy based on Plato and Aristotle, writers who drew upon Neoplatonic thought were again understood. Furthermore, the increasing rationalism of the twelfth century, particularly the use of Aristotle, meant an increasing dichotomy between rationality and nonrationalism, which meant that certain kinds of nonrational experience, hitherto considered natural, were placed by rationality in a special category of the supernatural. Internal illumination by the Spirit was primary among them.

Established order rightly sensed a danger to order in the millenarian idea that the age of theology was about to be replaced by the age of spiritual liberty. Still, the Fourth Lateran Council condemned only Joachim's criticisms of Peter Lombard's standard trinitarian theology, leaving his idea of the three ages uncondemned to bother theologians for centuries to come.

From the 1240s, Joachism would be tied with spiritually inclined Franciscans beginning with John of Parma, Minister General (1246–57), and Hugh of Digne (d. 1255). The alleged heresy that drew upon both Joachim and Amalric was the Heresy of the Free Spirit. These heretics never existed as a group except in the fantasy of the agents of order, who needed a category into which they could force a variety of people preaching antinomianism—the liberation of the individual from secular and ecclesiastical law by the power of the Holy Spirit. Once categorized, they could be assigned an amalgam of beliefs and practices (such as sexual license) that corresponded little with reality.

During the period from 1184 to 1250, the Waldensian and Cathar heresies both reached their highest influence, but they were gradually suppressed by bishops, popes, and secular leaders, who devised measures to identify dissenters, label them as heretics, and eliminate them. These countermeasures were greatly aided by the codification of doctrine and law by scholastic theologians and lawyers.

6

Institutional Response: 1250–1325

In the midthirteenth century, the methods of scholasticism dominated Western European thought in theology, philosophy, and civil
and canon law. Because the economic and demographic power of
the cities had increased, the universities, which had grown out of
the episcopal city schools of the twelfth century, had replaced the
monasteries as centers of thought. Modified philosophical Realism
held a near monopoly in the universities. This prevailing view was
Platonic Idealism strongly shaped by Aristotelian thought. The
greatest scholastics, the Dominicans Albert the Great (1200–80),
who wrote his *Summa theologiae* between 1270 and 1280, and his
younger and short-lived contemporary Thomas Aquinas (1226–74),
who began his in 1265, typified the Realists' belief that they could,
by reason enlightened by revelation, advance in some degree
toward absolute truth. This attitude in theology and law, expressing
itself in efforts to distinguish closely between truth and falsehood,
reinforced the tendency to distinguish sharply between orthodoxy
and heresy.

Thomas Aquinas and his contemporaries offered strict definitions of heresy: a heretic was one separated from the church by
deliberate rebellion and formation of a sect, or by persistent error
either in doctrine or in interpreting the Scriptures; or one who
rejects the sacraments or the authority of the bishops. But the
triumph of Aristotelian Realism in the 1250s and 1260s provoked a
reaction, and the University of Paris condemned some propositions

drawn from Aquinas himself. The condemnations of 1269, 1270, and especially 1277, condemned certain Aristotelian ideas and helped undermine Realism. Duns Scotus (1265–1308) and William of Ockham (1285–1347) showed the limits of rational discourse and were followed by theologians who have been called *nominalists*. Nominalists held that concepts or ideas such as "mountain," "king," or "angel" are merely human constructs that may tell us little or nothing about reality outside our own minds. By rejecting the search for absolute truth in theology through reason, this view encouraged *natural philosophy*—what is now called *science*—in the study of things as we observe them rather than as they "are" absolutely; it also encouraged the search for God through illumination by the Holy Spirit. This spirituality often expressed itself in personal and peculiar ways offensive to the defenders of order.

The university's condemnation of certain propositions is a matter of essential importance in the theory of how orthodoxy and heresy were separated. In the thirteenth and fourteenth centuries, the theoretical conflict became more sophisticated. The authority of the bishops was now explicitly challenged by the authority of the professors. The popes and bishops of the eleventh, twelfth, and early thirteenth centuries had built up a strong and effective claim to make that determination. But from the beginning of the thirteenth century, the universities grew increasingly independent of episcopal and papal control and began to set their own standards. By 1277, the bishop of Paris (Stephen Tempier) had to share with ad hoc commissions of scholars from the University of Paris the distinction of suppressing heretical ideas. The condemnation of that year aimed at separating theology, philosophy, and the arts in an effort to fragment the curriculum and to shift professional authority back to the bishops and to the governing bodies of the universities— what would now be called the administration. In the fourteenth century, universities increasingly took responsibility for "policing" their own faculties. They also set themselves on the side of order with the clear position that persistent refusal to accept the orthodox position on a topic was heretical. Fourteenth-century theologians such as William of Ockham and others attacked the bishops' intervention in the universities and pressed for even more autonomy for scholars.

Thus, academic errors as well as popular movements were considered real heresies. The universities came to regard *superbia* (pride) as the root of *curiositas* (idle search for knowledge for knowledge's sake). True knowledge could be obtained only with reference to tradition as set by the bishops—and the leaders of the universities. The idea of "freedom of thought" or "academic freedom" was a concept foreign to the fourteenth century.

Increased Repression

Thus the tension between dissent and orthodoxy increased. The means of repression begun at Verona in 1184 and formalized at the Fourth Lateran Council in 1215 were extended. In 1255, Alexander IV (1254–61) authorized summary or abbreviated procedures in a number of inquisitions, including ones for heresy. Alexander IV included not only heretics but also their "helpers" among those to be prosecuted, and a guilty verdict resulted in fines, penance, prison, or execution at the stake and confiscation of family property. Papal investigators such as Conrad of Marburg and Stephen of Bourbon (d. 1270) were busy in France, northern Italy, the Low Countries, and the Rhineland, investigating heresy from the cities to the most remote parishes. The major innovation of the century was allowing secret witnesses in some trials. The motive was to protect the witnesses, but the custom could only harm the defense. Still, all inquisitorial investigations, heretical or otherwise, assumed defendants innocent until a sufficient degree of proof had been established. Defendants were always entitled to legal counsel, although it was often difficult to find, for lawyers were afraid of persecution as "helpers" themselves.

Prosecution of heresies by the civil authorities increased rapidly through the thirteenth century. The Emperor Frederick II issued stern imperial decrees against heresy (the *Liber Augustalis*) in 1231. In 1239, Frederick broadened and tightened these measures, and they were accepted by Pope Innocent IV in 1252 as norms for secular laws against heresy. However, from the 1220s, Frederick's power was increasingly limited to southern Italy. Peter Diehl argues that from the 1230s the civil prosecution of heretics in the north was carried out by the newly independent Italian communes or city-states such as Milan and Verona, where mass executions for heresy began in 1233. By 1241, Moneta of Cremona was busily defending prosecution of heresy by the civil authorities. The reasons were two: the increasing power of the papacy and its determination to enforce orthodoxy, and the desire of the papacy to extend its political control over the urban communes of northern Italy. As the Lombard communes shifted their allegiance away from the emperor and toward the pope (who seemed a less efficient and therefore more desirable master), they tactfully incorporated papal legislation against heresies into their own municipal codes.

Until the end of the thirteenth century, then, investigations, including those against heresy, were on the whole restrained by judicial precedent and rules. But Boniface VIII's *Liber sextus* (1298) overturned some of the earlier restraints. Boniface permitted a judge to question witnesses before a formal charge against the defendant had been made. Confession by a suspect (under any circumstance, including threat of torture), was legally acceptable in lieu of a formal charge. This permitted judges to proceed against defendants without a formal list of charges against them. In heresy trials in particular, specific charges would be withheld from the defendant to see whether he would incriminate himself with his testimony. The move toward harsher procedures was less a change in the law itself than a change in practice, which became more permissive to the prosecution and less fair to the defendant. By the early fourteenth century, guidebooks for inquisitors were in circulation, such as the famous *Practica officii inquisitionis* (Manual of Inquisitors, 1322–23), by the investigator Bernard Gui.

Ordinarily either a confession or at least two eyewitnesses were needed to secure a conviction. Because eyewitnesses were often unavailable, the accused was pressured to confess, often under torture or threat of torture. The pastoral reason for this process was quite sincere: it was desirable for a heretic to confess and recant publicly for his or her own salvation and as a good example to the people. It was also reasonable in the eyes of the agents of order that the property of heretics should be appropriated to repay the community for the cost of their prosecution. When a suspect was formally accused, his or her property was sequestered and used to defray the costs of the trial. If he or she was convicted, it was permanently confiscated.

Such practices led to obvious abuses. The fiscal advantage to the authorities of confiscating the property of heretics presented a powerful impetus to loosen procedure, especially in a time of growing government with its attendant bureaucracy and need for revenue. From 1307 to 1312, King Philip IV of France persuaded Pope Clement V to help him frame false charges of heresy and sorcery against the leaders of the Templars, a semimonastic military order, to break their political power and obtain their property. Under a paranoid leader such as Pope John XXII, who saw enemies everywhere, official investigations could be used to root out any suspected enemy. Philip IV and Edward I of England (1307–27) drove the Jews out of their territories to plunder them. In the fourteenth and fifteenth centuries, secular rulers in Italy and Spain condemned and expelled Muslims and Jews as sons of Satan.

Heresy and the Contemplative Tradition

As the power of order in the Christian community increased, so did a deepening contemplative tradition on the opposite side. The contemplatives tended to believe that God was beyond human thought and all categories of any kind. God could be found, not through reason, but through prayer, seeking the light within. Two different perspectives also existed within the contemplative tradition. One was that God was at the core of the human soul, and in the deepest contemplation the soul encountered God closely, as in the Beatific Vision, the eternal bonding of the soul to God. The other, more radical, perspective was that at the very heart of the soul the distinction between God and human vanished and the two melded, the human becoming divine through being absorbed into Christ.

Although many of the greatest leaders of the church—such as Augustine, Pseudo-Dionysius, Bernard, and Francis—had embraced the contemplative tradition, the contemplatives' preference for the personal soul's encounter with God over rationalism and external authority left them open to suspicion. In the thirteenth and fourteenth centuries, contemplatives were frequently linked with dissent, partly because reliance upon internal inspiration led people to extremes; partly because the forces of order, mistrusting and fearing spirituality, labeled many varieties of it as heresy.

Such dissenters incorporated Reformist ideas, devaluing the sacramental priesthood and thus the entire authority of the ecclesiastical structure. They also tended toward millenarianism. As they were seldom organized, these dissenters were often called *beguins*, a term derived from the semimonastic houses (beguinages) of the Low Countries and possibly linked with Al*bigen*sians.[12] Although most of the beguinages remained impeccably orthodox, some of them were involved with Free Spirit ideas and the term *beguin* joined *publican* and *patarene* as a generic term for heresy.

Extreme expressions of contemplation linked with Joachim of Fiore leaped the bounds of orthodoxy. In 1254, Gerard of Borgo San Donnino wrote his *Introduction to the Eternal Gospel*, a distortion and exaggeration of Joachim's own ideas. The book claimed that the Third Age would appear in 1260, superseding the whole Second Age, including Christ and the Bible. For Gerard, Joachim was the new prophet; Joachim's books would be the Holy Scripture for the New Age. Here traditional Reformism was transformed: the idea was no longer the restoration or recreation of a pure apostolic past but rather a new irruption of the Divine into history so as to bring about a New (and Better) Age. This was pure millenarianism. The outbreak of the Flagellant movement at Perugia in 1260 probably occurred at that particular time because of Gerard's prophecy. Flagellants—usually men—publicly whipped themselves while singing psalms in order to atone for the sins of the world. The Flagellants were condemned but remained underground and scattered until the 1340s, when fear of the Black Death revived the movement. They were condemned again by Clement VI in 1349.

The failure of the New Age to materialize in 1260 slowed the movement only slightly; the date was merely moved forward to 1290, and then again as needed. Having committed themselves so thoroughly to a sect from which their lives derived meaning, many sectaries were undeterred when a specific prophecy failed to materialize.

The Apostolici, or Apostolic Brethren, founded by Gerardo Segarelli in 1260, thought that the New Age would be ushered in by a return to apostolic purity within their own sect. The Apostolici upstaged the Franciscans, the *fratres minores* (lesser brothers), by calling themselves the *fratres minimi* (least brothers); the Franciscans on their side denounced the Apostolici as illiterate intruders into their own constituency. The Council of Lyon in 1274, following the Fourth Lateran Council in condemning all new orders, ordered the Apostolici to disband. They refused, and Segarelli was eventually burned in 1300.

Conventuals and Spirituals

The popularity of the Franciscans attracted gifts of land and property and responsibilities for preaching and education that drew them away from Francis's original vision of poverty. Bonaventure, Minister General of the Order from 1257 to 1274, wrote a work *Apologia pauperum* arguing that although Franciscans might not own property they might "use" it for charitable purposes, a view explicitly approved by Pope Nicholas III (1277–80). Bonaventure believed that absolute poverty was a counsel of perfection, that is, a desirable but not a necessary trait in a Franciscan friar. He drew upon the Bible to show that the apostles held possessions, and he argued from the tradition of the church and the recent tradition of the Franciscan Order to show that the holding of property was not necessarily evil and could be used for good purposes. For Bonaventure, preaching and teaching were so essential to the order that poverty became only one among the items in the Franciscan program. But Bonaventure's effort to obtain a consensus on this middle ground failed.

Peter-John Olivi (c. 1248–98), a Franciscan from Narbonne in the midst of old Albigensian country, upheld against Bonaventure the *usus pauper*, the doctrine of strict adherence to Francis's stipulation that his followers own nothing. This difference led to a sharp divergence within the order between the Conventuals, who followed Bonaventure, and the Spirituals, who followed Olivi. Olivi annoyed the Conventuals by attempting to make the usus pauper a legal as well as moral requirement by making it part of the vow of poverty. Following Hugh of Digne, Olivi's *usus pauper* entailed ragged clothing, no shoes, no horses, no money, and reliance upon begging.

The Spirituals, rather than bothering with the Conventuals' versions of Francis's life even by glossing them or correcting them, evolved their own oral tradition, eventually written down in books such as *The Little Flowers of Saint Francis*. The Spirituals' works, which emphasized Francis's original poverty, were efforts to construct a new tradition. Whether naively or astutely, they created texts to back their own interpretation.

The Conventuals' rejection of such standards provoked Olivi, and he began to be attracted by Joachism. He wrote a commentary on the Apocalypse, the *Postilla super apocalypsim*, which drew heavily on Joachim's teaching (and was condemned by John XXII in 1326). Although there had been many previous commentaries on the Book of Revelation, never before Joachim had anyone set it in historical terms relating to contemporary events. Olivi argued that Francis had initiated a New Age of the Spirit characterized by internal illumination. That age would culminate in the liberty of all souls to unite with God; but this happy consummation was to be preceded by a millenarian period during which the iniquitous would persecute the just, by which Olivi meant the Conventuals' persecution of the Spirituals. The rejected minority, faithful to Francis, perceived the Conventuals and their backers in the papal government as followers of the Evil One.

The Conventuals had the backing of the papacy and so tended to view the Spirituals as dissenters. Some of the Conventuals moved farther toward materialism. This in turn impelled some Spirituals further to emphasize internal revelation against ecclesiastical authority and moved them toward an unrestrained spirituality that pushed the boundaries of orthodoxy. These radical Spirituals became known as the Fraticelli (little brothers), and they were linked by their enemies with the beguins. The Fraticelli were themselves divided into a number of dissonant groups, but they tended to slide in the direction of millenarianism.

The division between the two groups of Franciscans was formalized by the Council of Lyon in 1274, and when Olivi died in 1298, the antagonism only worsened. Olivi's views were carried forward with more zeal and extravagance by his follower Ubertino de Casale (1259–1330), whose views are most clearly expressed in his book *Arbor vitae, The Tree of Life*. Ubertino perceived the Spirituals' opponents as the Antichrist. In 1312, at the Council of Vienne, Pope Clement V issued *Exivi de paradiso* and *Fidei catholicae fundamento*, decrees supporting a moderate version of the Spirituals' position. But his successor, Pope John XXII (1316–34), replaced Clement's decrees with a very hostile one of his own, *Quorumdam exigit* (1317). Despite John's efforts to eradicate the Spirituals, they remained active, especially in Provence and Lombardy. The Spiritual Angelo da Clareno (c. 1320) declared that John XXII and Emperor Frederick II were the followers of Antichrist who now at the end of the world was rallying the forces of evil. The split in the Franciscan Order was never healed in the Middle Ages.

Meanwhile, after the death of Gerardo Segarelli, Dolcino, a semiliterate priest's son, had become the leader of the Apostolici. In 1300, he issued a manifesto declaring that he had received a direct revelation from the Holy Spirit: the papacy was false; most priests and popes were sinners; the Apostolici were the *true* church. Again, a heretical group deliberately defined itself out of the Catholic church, a move imitated later by the Hussites and then by the

Protestants. The Spirit also revealed to Dolcino that the New Age would begin when everyone adopted the apostolic life; this united the Apostolici in sympathy (though not in organization) with the Spirituals. In 1303, Dolcino announced that he had gained 4,000 adherents. The Apostolici attracted horrified opposition from the Conventuals and the defenders of order, who saw in such ideas a reproach and a threat to their claim to represent Christian tradition. The prophetess Guglielma of Milan was also influenced by the Apostolici. Her followers venerated her after her death as the incarnation of the Holy Spirit and the initiator of the New Age. The Guglielmites were led by Manfreda, who called herself pope and surrounded herself with female cardinals. Guglielma, who died in 1281, was disinterred and burnt for heresy in 1300. Dolcino was executed in 1307.

Women played a special role in dissent in the early church and again from Theuda in the ninth century to Guglielma in the thirteenth. In Catharism and other sects they were more nearly equal to men than in Catholicism. Women had more influence in the sects than in the Catholic church because they were allowed to claim and exercise an authority denied Catholic women (except abbesses and prioresses). With the rise of simple literacy and the spread of apostolic ideals to the population as a whole, women with a calling to the religious life could no longer all be absorbed by the orthodox monasteries. Monasteries for women had limited resources and usually demanded a dowry when a woman entered the house, and many of the newly inspired women were from poor families. They found that poverty was excluding them from the religious life; they found this an anomaly if not a scandal, and they began creating new contemplative houses of their own. Unfortunately they did so after new orders had been forbidden by the decrees of 1215 and 1274. In the later Middle Ages, women became more prominent among the Spirituals and the beguins.

Antinomianism

The unregulated spiritual and millennial movements of the thirteenth century produced heterodox ideas linked to the vague terms *beguin* and *Free Spirit* and revolving around the notion that personal illumination by the Holy Spirit was an authority superior to any human law or rule. Although condemnations of beguins began in the thirteenth century, they came to a head in the fourteenth, beginning with the case of Marguerite Porete of Hainaut, condemned as a heretic about 1306. Marguerite wrote a basic spiritual book, *The Mirror of Simple Souls,* a dispute between Love and Reason over a human soul. The book describes seven stages of perfection of a soul moving toward God. Stages of spiritual perfection (especially seven stages) were a commonplace of spiritual writing, and *The Mirror* was accepted as orthodox by many monastic houses. Still, its success frightened the agents of order. The seventh stage, the Beatific Vision, the bonding of the soul with God, could only be accomplished in eternity, so it posed no difficulties for established order. But the fifth and sixth stages did, because they linked with Joachism: in these stages the Holy Spirit progressively releases the Christian from the necessity of obedience to all earthly law. At its root the idea is found in Augustine's "love and do what you will." In other words, one who is filled with Christian love has already responded to Christ's grace with faith; he or she will inevitably do good works for love, not law. But the church had always for pastoral reasons downplayed this point of view, and in any event Marguerite expressed it crudely. In her sixth state, which can be reached on earth, the human soul becomes like an angel, standing free in God's presence without intermediary.

Antinomianism became the hallmark of heresies labeled as *beguin* or *Free Spirit.* In 1307, Henry of Virneburg, Archbishop of Cologne, condemned radical Spirituals as beguins whose views could lead to the rejection of the sacraments, laws, and the authority of the bishops. Henry's condemnation was followed by a far more influential one, *Ad nostrum,* a decree issued by the Council of Vienne in 1312 under the leadership of Pope Clement V. The council considered ordering the complete suppression of all beguins on the grounds of unauthorized preaching, but it ended by specifically charging certain beguins in Germany for believing that a human being can become perfect and incapable of sin, that such persons, having become perfect, can do as they please, and that they are above the laws of church and state.

These charges, doubtless exaggerated, nonetheless contained some truth. The Cathar perfects had claimed superiority to the law, and many Contemplatives believed that one could become perfect by the grace and power of the Holy Spirit within. A few extravagant Contemplatives crudely misunderstood such theology and believed that they stood above the law; that everything they did was right because the Spirit did it in them. Clement V was the same pope who helped Philip IV condemn the Templars, and his successor John XXII was irrationally terrified of heretics, witches, and poisoners. From the beginning John took a hostile attitude toward the Spirituals as threats to papal authority. John XXII's decree *Quorumdam exigit* selectively drew from Clement's V's *Exivi de paradiso* in order to emphasize the right of pope and council to define the proper degree of poverty required under the Franciscan Rule. Because many Spirituals refused to recognize either this right or the validity of the pope's interpretations, they were prosecuted, and in 1318 four were burned at Marseille as heretics. John XXII's decree *Sancta romana* (1317) was aimed against the Fraticelli and the beguins and anyone who helped or supported them. In 1323 John issued the decree *Cum inter nonnullos,* which condemned the Spirituals' view of poverty and claimed that Christ and the apostles approved of private property. These decrees, along with John's condemnation of Olivi's book on the apocalypse in 1326, drove the Spirituals to even more radical opposition to order.

Papal decrees were echoed by local authorities. John of Dürbheim, Archbishop of Strasbourg, launched a prosecution of "Free Spirits" on the grounds that they were antinomians and pantheists and that they believed in universalism (the idea that because everyone originates with God, everyone will return to God and be saved). In Cologne about 1340, John of Brunn confessed to having been a beguin whose confidence in the Freedom of the Spirit permitted him to lie, fornicate, murder, have orgies, and to commit incest, sodomy, and infanticide. Such charges were beginning to be made against "witches" as well. Some fanatics actually believed and practiced such things, but their numbers and organization (if any) were exaggerated by the frightened authorities. The confession of John Hartmann at Erfurt in 1367 included the approval of incest, even upon the altar, along with the convenient doctrine that a woman could regain her lost virginity by fornicating with one of the Free Spirits. Again, it is difficult to judge whether John's confession was coerced and therefore whether there was any truth in it. Prosecution of beguins and Free Spirits declined by the end of the century, partly because the prosecution of "witches" was displacing it. The last prosecution of Free Spirits was in Germany in 1458.

In the later Middle Ages, the Contemplative tradition spread in movements of popular piety where laypeople drew upon the ideals of monastic contemplation while remaining in the home and at work. Jan Ruysbroeck (1293–1381), a regular canon, was one of the founders of the popular *Devotio moderna,* and drawing on this spirit, Geert de Groote (1340–84), a scholar turned mystic and monk, founded the Brethren of the Common Life, which eventually produced the popular Contemplative writer on lay spirituality Thomas à Kempis (1380–1471). These movements remained within the borders of orthodoxy because they emphasized the centrality of the Eucharist and the necessity of an ordained priesthood. They nevertheless provided a center of spiritual power separate from the normal sources of order.

This is an important point for understanding the opposition of many groups to orthodox Eucharistic theology in general and to transubstantiation in particular. To attack the ability of the priest to make Christ present on the altar and to distribute validly consecrated bread and wine is to undermine the clerical claim to be the only mediators of salvation.

The most famous of the radical Contemplatives to be condemned was Meister Eckhart. Although Eckhart preached against the beguins himself, his own views, like those of the other Rhenish mystics, Suso and Tauler, were linked with antinomianism. Just before his death in 1327, Eckhart's views were prosecuted by Henry of Virneburg, Archbishop of Cologne, and 28 propositions taken from his works were condemned by John XXII in the decree *In agro dominico* (1329).

The period from 1250 to 1325 was marked by the absence of powerful popular heresies such as the Cathars before or the Hussites later, an absence partly owing to the effective measures of repression installed by the forces of order. Nonetheless, ancient ideas about the apocalypse and about the sanctity of voluntary poverty were revived in new forms and, especially in their influence among the Spirituals, posed a new challenge to order by dissent.

The focus of attention was already beginning to change. The fourteenth century witnessed the origins of a new variety of dissent, the evangelical heresies of the Wyclifites and Hussites, who combined previous Reformist views of apostolic poverty and preaching with a new emphasis upon the text of the Bible and the duty of devout Christians to read it for themselves.

7

Evangelical Heresy: 1325–1437

In many ways the new evangelical movements of Wycliffites, Lollards, and Hussites were similar to previous medieval dissent, but in other ways they resembled the future Protestant Reformation. The period from 1350 to 1650 is best seen as a unity where the old Reformist movements were transformed by the evangelical emphasis on the Bible, by the moral programs of the Renaissance humanists, and by the power of the civil authorities, who reasserted their rights as guardians of order to a higher degree than in the early Middle Ages.

The history of heresy changes radically from the fourteenth century on, but at least some of the change may be in the minds of modern historians. The idea of "precursors" of the Protestant Reformation is only one example of an explanation imposed on events. To read most histories of dissent, one would think that earlier forms of heresies had ceased to exist when John Wyclif and Jan Hus appeared. In fact many continued, including the Waldensians (in a minor way), the Fraticelli and Joachites (in a major way), and the radical mystics. Historians, being intellectuals, tend to overestimate the intellectual elements in a situation. Because Wyclif and Hus were both intellectuals with well-defined systems, many historians have been tempted to downplay the serious economic and political elements involved in the heresies. Others more recently have in reaction overemphasized these elements at the expense of the intellectual. A balance needs to be found.

As for order and dissent, the evangelical dissenters added to the typical medieval challenges against order by elevating the biblical text above bishops, tradition, and reason alike.

The development of these new movements of dissent and their repression as heresies related to important political and social shifts in the later Middle Ages. One was the expansion of urban culture with the accompanying concentration of wealth, power, and literacy among the upper middle class (wealthy merchants and industrialists) and increasing literacy and self-assertion among artisans. A second was the growing power of temporal princes such as the kings of England and France, the upper German nobility, and the leaders of the Italian city-states. A third, related closely to the second, was the corruption of ecclesiastical property by the bishops or the civil authorities, who exploited pluralism of benefices, assigning many parishes to one priest (who was unable to serve them all properly) and pocketing the savings to maintain expanding bureaucracies. A fourth was the beginning of ethnic and linguistic nationalism, which fostered, and was fostered by, increasing secular authority. A fifth was the decline of papal prestige and authority owing to the Great Schism (1378–1417), when two or sometimes three popes vied with one another for recognition by the secular rulers.

A sixth was the growing power of conciliarism, which accompanied the decline of papal prestige. Led by theologians, canon lawyers, and political theorists, the conciliarists argued for a return to a more community-oriented concept of the church—a new emphasis upon the authority of the bishops assembled in council as opposed to that of a papal monarch. Papal monarchy had been an innovation of the eleventh century to which the conciliarists were now objecting. By raising the question of the true nature of the church and the source of authority, the conciliarists opened the door to more radical ideas. These included the religious dissent of the Wycliffites and Hussites and new emphasis on political theories that held that authority flows up from the people rather than down from pope or emperor.

Seventh, the spread of education beyond clerical circles to the Christian population as a whole, at least in the cities, led to increased intolerance of ignorant or corrupt clergy. Corruption certainly existed in the late medieval church, but probably no more than at any other time. But the more literate and knowledgeable the urban population became, the less they were willing to tolerate clerical incompetence and corruption. Ironically, orthodox zeal to criticize and correct corruption led to a wider perception of, and intolerance of, incompetence, so that orthodox reform prompted reform dissent. The dissatisfaction of unbeneficed clergy—priests without parishes—added to dissent.

Finally, the fourteenth century experienced severe social unrest owing to the unusual number and severity of famines and plagues, and the social and economic dislocations they caused, culminating most luridly in the peasants' rebellion in France in 1358, the *Jacquerie*, and the peasants' revolt of 1381 in England. Social dislocations played a part in the new dissent. England and Bohemia were regions previously marginal in medieval dissent, without elaborate systems of repression, and the particularly strong nationalism in those countries may have aided dissent. In Bohemia, the occasional support of the king and the continued support of many nobles added to Hussite strength.

John Wyclif

The leader of the English dissent, John Wyclif (c. 1330–84), came from Yorkshire but spent most of his life at Oxford, where he was Master of Balliol from 1360 to 1361. He left Oxford permanently only in 1381, shortly before his death. Although earlier medieval academics such as Abelard or Amalric had small popular followings, and Wyclif during his lifetime had a number of followers, Wyclif was the first academic dissenter whose ideas inspired a widespread popular movement after his death. Wycliffism was a potent combination of intellectual concepts, moral reformism, and popular resentment.

Philosophically an Aristotelian Realist, Wyclif defended the existence of Universals—eternal and unchangeable thoughts in the mind of God that could be at least dimly understood by human reason. This influenced his sacramental theology. Wyclif, like orthodox theologians, accepted transubstantiation, the view that the bread and wine change at the Eucharist into the Body and Blood of Christ. Wyclif's views were Aristotelian, but he rejected the views of Aquinas, which maintained that the bread became Christ's Body in essence though not in quantity (a technical term asserting that on one level it remained bread), and the views of Ockham that the bread and wine disappeared at the moment of consecration, becoming completely Christ's Body and Blood. Wyclif argued that the elements after consecration fully became Christ's Body and Blood but also remained bread and wine both in essence and attribute, a position prefiguring Martin Luther's doctrine of consubstantiation and concentrating on "spiritual" rather than "physical" change. The view was on the border of orthodoxy in the fourteenth century, and many thought it heretical.

More important was Wyclif's ecclesiology. He saw the rising power of the prince as a counterweight to the authority of the bishops and pope and hoped to use the temporal powers—the king and nobles—to pressure the church into reform. The temporal powers, for their part, found Wyclif's academic influence and popular appeal useful tools against ecclesiastical power and property. Wyclif's doctrine of disendowment, renunciation of wealth by the church, had attracted needy (or greedy) nobles. Duke John of Gaunt made use of Wyclif during the 1370s, securing him against prosecution, but later, when Wyclif had become too radical and when the political situation had changed, abandoned him. As Luther did later, Wyclif eventually became frightened of the use to which his ideas were being put by popular extremists and issued a condemnation of the peasants' revolt of 1381. Excommunicated in 1377, he made a *Confession* in 1381 that reaffirmed his basic doctrines. In 1382, Archbishop William Courtenay of Canterbury "purged" Wyclif's sympathizers from Oxford University, and Wyclif died in 1384 unreconciled with ecclesiastical order. His works were formally condemned by Archbishop Arundel in 1411, and in 1428 his body was exhumed and removed from sanctified ground.

Wyclif was the most prolific writer of all medieval dissenters.[13] He argued that the church of the apostles was a church of voluntary poverty, contrasting it with the wealth and worldly power of the contemporary clergy, which, he claimed, had abandoned the apostolic ideal. Because the moral corruption of the church stemmed from its attachment to wealth, he argued for disendowment, the voluntary renunciation by the church of all goods not specifically and clearly needed to carry on the work of Christ. This idea, rejected by the ecclesiastical leadership, prompted Wyclif to reformulate an ancient radical view of the very nature of the church.

The true church was not, he claimed, the "visible" church represented by the bishops and other officers of order and their followers; rather it was the "invisible" community of all those whom Christ has saved. Most clergy were morally unfit. Humanity

was divided into the elect (those chosen by Christ as his community, his mystical Body), and those not chosen and known in
eternity (*presciti*) by God to be incapable of salvation. A *prescitus*
could not be a valid priest, but on the other hand no mortal could
know whether a given priest was *prescitus* or one of the elect. Wyclif
specifically rejected the idea that the bishops know this, for their
behavior and that of many of their clergy raised doubts as to their
own salvation. Because a priest could not be known to be a true
priest, the rationale for the priesthood vanished. For Wyclif,
priesthood inhered in all true believers. In 1377, his views were
condemned by Gregory XII, and he then came to regard the entire
hierarchy as the Antichrist.

This radical view of the priesthood was accompanied by a
daring reassessment of the Eucharist. Wyclif's view of the clergy led
him to a kind of Donatism (where sacraments administered by
corrupt clergy are suspect). He never, unlike some of his followers,
denied the Real Presence of Christ in the Eucharist, but he did
argue that there was no way of defining that presence. By 1379, he
was specifically denying the doctrine of transubstantiation eluci-
dated by Thomas Aquinas and other scholastics. To Wyclif, the
argument that the essences of bread and wine were replaced by the
essences of Body and Blood while retaining all the attributes of
bread and wine was unacceptable. This move alienated many of his
academic and clerical followers, including his colleagues at Oxford
and his supporters among the friars who had commended his views
on poverty. Around 1379 he published a treatise, *De potestate* (*On
Power*), which denied the authority of the pope and the cardinals. A
commission at Oxford condemned his views in 1380–81, and when
he issued his *Confession* in 1381, reaffirming his denial of transubstantiation, he had to leave the university.

In rejecting the authority of the bishops, Wyclif implicitly
rejected the authority of the tradition of which they were the
guardians. Wyclif was also suspicious both of internal illumination
and reason. Thus he turned to the Bible as the highest authority.
This represented a fundamental shift in the Christian concept of
authority, provoking a dispute that would come to a head in the
Protestant Reformation.

Wyclif's treatise *De veritate sacre scripture* (*On the Truth of Holy
Scripture*), c. 1377, proclaimed the infallibility of the Bible; every
word was eternally true; later he modified this to say that the
underlying *sense* of the words was eternally true. The Bible was the

work of God and must be taken in all of its parts without qualification. The Bible was to be understood not necessarily by professors and prelates but by the individual Christian reading it prayerfully with the help of the Holy Spirit. Wyclif's followers Nicholas of Hereford and John Purvey, encouraged by rising English nationalism, undertook an English translation of large portions of the Bible. Vernacular translations of parts of the Bible had previously existed but were intended for devotional purposes among wealthy and influential laypeople; the new translation was intended for as wide an audience as possible. All literate people should, the Wycliffites believed, have a Bible to read for themselves and to the illiterate.

For Wyclif the dichotomy had become clear. On the one side was God and the Bible; on the other side was Satan and the pope. However, Wyclif's antipapalism was in no way Joachite or apocalyptic, since he wished to build a true church on earth with the aid of the secular powers. Lay support of Wyclif was widespread. At first, in the 1370s, nobles such as Duke John of Gaunt, attracted by his disendowment principle, helped him. But after Wyclif's 1381 *Confession,* and above all because of their uneasiness at the peasants' revolt (which Wyclif was still held partly accountable for though he had condemned it), the higher nobility withdrew their support, permitting Courtenay's purge at the 1382 Blackfriars' Synod. The peasants' revolt, though its roots were economic, not religious, did draw upon some Wycliffite rhetoric, and in any event it frightened off some of Wyclif's followers among the gentry.

The Lollards

The break between Wyclif and his clerical and academic supporters between 1379 and 1381, and the growth of his teachings among the middle class and poor, gained him a wide popular following known as *Lollards* (a pejorative term derived from a Low German word for "babbler"). Academic Wycliffites driven from Oxford University by the purge of 1382, for example Philip Repton, a friar, and Nicholas of Hereford, a secular priest, preached in chapels, approved lay preachers, and distributed tracts. They taught that all Christians were equal, that none had dominion over others, and that all had a right to preach. Because less educated preachers comprised a greater proportion of the leadership, Lollard views gradually became less sophisticated and more extreme. Some of the intellectual leaders recanted and returned to orthodoxy and obedience, partly out of fear of reprisals and partly because of the radicalization of Lollard doctrine. Even Wyclif's personal secretary, John Purvey, recanted in 1401.

Lollardy continued to be an intellectual heresy. Still, many uneducated people also held views bordering on Lollardy: contempt for absentee priests, the plurality of benefices, and the luxurious behavior of prelates. As the Lollards were increasingly cut off from the clergy and the university, the sociology of the group changed. There were fewer gentry, fewer clergy, fewer merchants, while there were more poorly educated craftsmen and artisans. This both compounded the doctrinal radicalism and substantially reduced the political power of the movement. (Anne Hudson has argued against exaggerating this shift.)

The Lollards took an extreme position on the Eucharist: the bread and wine were not transubstantiated into Body and Blood; clergy were unnecessary, for anyone could consecrate the Eucharist; prayerful reading of Scripture under the guidance of the Spirit was the essence of Christianity, so the Eucharist was not central to Christian worship. They set aside the church fathers and ecumenical councils along with the pope and the bishops. Some Lollards believed that the Bible alone held all the truth and alone was the source of all salvation.

The emphasis upon preaching, primarily from the Bible, was the chief characteristic of Lollardy and separated it from its origins in intellectual Wycliffism, for which the written word was still preeminent. But the connection remained, as services were often held in church, although Lollards were safer with services in private homes with a more fluid liturgy (the Eucharist being celebrated or not depending on the congregation's degree of radicalism) with a sermon in English and often much participation by the people. The purpose of the sermon was to convey the power of the Bible directly and (allegedly) unencumbered by interpretation to the people, although opponents rightly saw that no text can be read without interpretation. Lollard vernacular sermons were characterized by exclusive reference to scriptural texts without reference to patristic or scholastic commentaries or to *exempla* (collections of sermon materials popular among late medieval clergy).

Extremism and isolation fed each other, and the Lollards were increasingly subject to prosecution. The 1401 English civil statute *De haeretico comburendo* ordered the execution of convicted Lollards; William Sawtrey was the first Lollard to be burned under the statute. Religious and political resistance combined in the rebellion of Sir John Oldcastle, one of the last of the gentry to support the Lollards. Arrested for heresy in 1413, Oldcastle defied the authority of the bishops. His rebellion died out in 1414; it had only confirmed temporal leaders' support of the bishops in putting down a movement that was politically as well as theologically disruptive. The situation was quite different later with the Hussites and later still with the Protestants, both of whom found substantial temporal support. By contrast, King Henry V in 1414 required secular judges to inquire into the existence of heretics—Lollards—in their jurisdictions and to prosecute them. After 1414, Lollardy ceased to be a politically or publicly important movement, although Lollard groups and individuals persisted into the 1530s, after which they merged into Protestantism.

The doctrines of the Lollards became more radical as prosecutions became more severe. The idea of the Antichrist revived as the Lollards came to see themselves as persecuted saints tormented by the forces of evil. The idea of Antichrist went back to the church fathers, who mostly saw the Antichrist as a corporate designation for all who opposed Christ, though a few fathers thought of him as an individual or as a group of individuals. Adso of Montier-en-Der in the twelfth century introduced the idea of the Antichrist as a specific person, describing his life in reverse hagiographical terms, making every saintly quality an evil. The Antichrist, the servant of Satan, would appear near the end of the world to lead the forces of evil in a last hopeless battle against the followers of Christ. After the battle, Christ himself would bring the world to an end and rule in eternity. Adso's view was spread by Honorius Augustodunensis (early twelfth century), whose *Elucidarium* was widely disseminated and translated into both French and English. The *Elucidarium* also supported the radical view that unworthy priests could not consecrate.

The Lollard view modified these precedents considerably: the saved (mainly the Lollards) were the invisible church, the elect, the body of Christ, whereas the damned were the body of the Antichrist. The Antichrists were the pope and the papal court, the bishops, the monks—all those who upheld traditional order. Such a view was to occur again in Hussitism and later in Protestantism. Some editions of the "Authorized" or "King James" version of the

Bible are still printed with a commentary describing the pope as the Antichrist.

The connection of the Lollards—or at least of Wyclif—with the Bohemian Reform was direct, owing to Richard II's marriage with Anne of Bohemia. Wyclif's ideas at Oxford University were transferred to the University of Prague through a wide net of Wycliffite or semi–Wycliffite ideas through many European universities, especially in Paris and Germany. They were discussed and widely adopted at the University of Prague. There they became a major component in the Bohemian Reform Movement, along with the legacy of heresy from the early Middle Ages. What made the Bohemian Reform Movement stronger than the English is that first Bohemian nobles and then a wide section of the Bohemian populace both in the cities and in the country supported the heresy as a manifestation of Czech nationalism against their German-speaking rulers.

The Hussites

The Czech reform movement is usually known as Hussitism, although Jan Hus (1372–1415) was only one of a number of its leaders and not the most important; it was his execution by the Council of Constance in 1415 that lent his name to the movement. The movement began gradually and within orthodoxy. King Charles IV (1346–78) was a sophisticated and educated ruler of the House of Luxembourg, which briefly dominated the Holy Roman Empire. Charles made Prague an intellectual and artistic center and founded the University of Prague in 1348, inviting Reform-minded Augustinian Canons onto the faculty. Charles was strongly orthodox, issuing decrees against beguins, and he had no idea that his reform measures would lead to heresy. He nevertheless unwittingly prepared the way, because with his French connections he supported the Avignon papacy in mandating papal appointment of bishops and abbots, thus depriving the nobility of one of its traditional sources of power and wealth and alienating it from both the papacy and the monarchy.

Charles's chaplain and confessor, Conrad Waldhauser, preached against the financial abuses of the bishops and of the monasteries, supporting the reform and papal positions, but further alienating the nobility. Waldhauser, who died in 1369, was the spiritual forefather of the Bohemian Reform Movement, for he influenced a canon of the cathedral of Prague, Jan Milič, to become a radical. Milič argued for poverty and asceticism on the grounds of biblical authority and attacked Charles IV himself as a supporter of an old order that was soon to perish with the coming of the Antichrist and the Last Battle. Preaching in Czech as well as in Latin, Milič reached beyond clerical and academic circles to the urban middle class, which, in addition to sincere concern for reform, desired the church's wealth to be diverted into commercially useful channels.

Milič in turn influenced Matthias of Janov, a scholar who provided the theoretical basis for the Bohemian Reform Movement. Matthias wrote 12 rules of conduct derived, not from monastic or conciliar roots, but directly from the Bible, and he suggested that the visible church was the Antichrist as opposed to the true church composed of those practicing evangelical piety. Nonetheless, Matthias still saw a function for the clergy, for he emphasized the importance of the Eucharist and advocated frequent reception of Communion by the laity.

The tendency to identify the visible church with evil increased with the Great Schism. It was easy to identify one papal claimant or another as the Antichrist and only a step from there to make the papacy itself an Antichrist. The emphasis of the Reformers shifted from reforming the papacy to questioning it, limiting it, or eventually even ignoring or abolishing it. The Great Schism also undermined the ability of order to suppress dissent where it arose.

Charles IV was succeeded by Wenceslas IV (1378–1419), a king who changed his views according to expediency. Struggling for political power against a factious Czech nobility, Wenceslas initially had no time for monitoring theological disputes. As to the church, he was concerned mainly with deciding whether it was more expedient to support the papacy at Rome or the papacy at Avignon. His intent was to use the papal split to enhance royal control over the bishops and monasteries, thereby reserving to himself revenues that under Charles IV had gone to the pope.

At this point Wyclif's ideas were penetrating Prague University, with the German masters on the whole opposing them but the Czech masters supporting them. The old hostility between the politically dominant German minority in Bohemia and the dissatisfied Czech majority thus began to have a religious side, preparing the way for a union of Bohemian nationalism with Bohemian dissent. In the reign of Wenceslas, the Reform movement transmuted into dissent and finally into heresy. One of the initial supporters of Wycliffism was Stanislav of Znojmo, who wrote the treatise *De corpore Christi, On the Body of Christ*, supporting Wyclif's radical view of the Eucharist. Later, Stanislav would turn against the dissenters. In 1408, Archbishop Zbyněk launched a determined assault on Wycliffism in the university, but his efforts failed.

Meanwhile a young professor at the university was rising to the fore: Jan Hus. From a peasant family, Hus took his Master's degree at Prague in 1396. Sometime before 1400, he had a conversion experience and embraced the teachings of Wyclif and the reformers. He was ordained a priest in 1400 and became dean of the faculty of philosophy in 1401. As rector of the Bethlehem Chapel, a reform foundation where he preached in Czech to vast congregations, Hus followed Milič's example of spreading reform ideas far beyond the university. For 12 years at Bethlehem, Hus preached thousands of sermons combining reform theology with Czech nationalism, insisting that Czechs, as the majority, should have control over university, church, and temporal power in Bohemia. In 1411, one of the three papal claimants, "John XXIII", excommunicated him and in 1412 placed his followers under interdict. Hus's 1413 treatise *De ecclesia, On the Church*, strongly influenced by Wyclif, challenged ecclesiastical order to a degree that order found intolerable, although Hus always tried to work within the framework of the church's unity and never intended to break off from the Catholic church.

Meanwhile, the politics of the schism had led King Wenceslas in 1409 to shift his own position. It suited him to support the conciliar movement and to play to Czech nationalism. Because the Czech faculty at the university tended to support conciliarism while the Germans opposed it, the king issued the 1409 decree, *Kutná Hora*, changing the voting structure at the university so as to give the Czechs the more powerful position. These Czech conciliarist professors were also the strongest supporters of Wycliffism, but Wenceslas was uninterested in protecting orthodox theology—or indeed any theology. The king and the reformers entered into an informal alliance, and in this setting Hus, with his immense popular following at the Bethlehem Chapel, rose to a position of leadership of the Reform party. His brilliant oratory and his honest and uncompromising position against clerical abuses won him the rectorship of the university in 1409, and with royal support he was able to thwart Zbyněk's effort to reestablish orthodox order. Defeated, Zbyněk resigned as archbishop in 1410 and went into exile.

For a while king, reformers, and Czech nationalists found common ground, but as the king had no interest in either reform or nationalism except insofar as they were useful to him, the pattern did not endure. In 1412, Wenceslas, hearing that reformers were publicly condemning and protesting a sale of royally approved indulgences in the cathedral, feared that the dissenters were breeding contempt for temporal as well as spiritual order. When the protestors refused to submit, he ordered them arrested and executed.

This coercion pushed some of the dissenters farther. In 1412, Nicholas of Dresden (d. 1416), who led a radical group of theologians, published his book *Tabule veteris et novi coloris, Tables of the Old and the New Color,* the old "color" of apostolic poverty being contrasted with the new "color" of the wealthy clergy. As the old color represented the Body of Christ, so the new color represented the Antichrist. Nicholas blurred the distinction between honest and corrupt clergy and condemned ecclesiastical order as a whole, including the priesthood, the Eucharist, purgatory, the cult of the saints, and the use of images. Using tracts and (ironically) pictures to spread his views, Nicholas obtained a wide popular following.

At this time Jakoubek of Stríbro, a professor at Prague, began to gain attention. Influenced by Matthias of Janov's emphasis upon frequency of lay communion, Jakoubek went much farther. He demanded that the custom of the ancient church that laypeople receive the Eucharist under both species (bread and wine) be revived. Hus and other reformers were inclined to take a mild view on this position, known as *Utraquism,* from the Latin meaning "both." But Jakoubek insisted that the Eucharist was valid only if administered under both species and that priests refusing to do so were damned. This radicalism fit his declaration that the pope was Antichrist and that the Holy Spirit had in disgust abandoned the Catholic church. Jakoubek's influence rose when Hus was exiled from Prague in July 1412, and by 1414 he was attempting to enforce utraquism on the Czech clergy. Hus refused to agree that communion under both species was necessary until just before his execution in 1415.

Hus's views on the nature of the church appear in his debates with Stanislav of Znojmo and Jan Páleč in 1412 and 1413. Znojmo, who had supported the reform party, now found their dissent too extreme. Hus's *De ecclesia* followed Wyclif in teaching that the true church was the invisible community of the saved and that the papacy should be rejected; nonbiblical and nonapostolic, it had begun only in the fourth century under the patronage of the Roman emperors. But by continuing to proclaim the validity of the Eucharist and of clerical celebration of the Eucharist, Hus took too moderate a line for some of the dissenters.

However, his line was too radical for the king. In 1415, Wenceslas, threatened by the dissenters' continued challenge to his authority, made an agreement with his brother King Sigismund of Germany (1410–37) by which Sigismund summoned Hus to the Council of Constance under a "safe conduct," allegedly to present his ideas, thus removing Hus's subversive influence from Wenceslas's kingdom. The safe conduct was flagrantly violated and Hus burnt at the stake in 1415. The execution of Hus at Constance after he refused to recant did not, however, help Wenceslas at all. Instead, it provoked a formal protest from the Czech nobility, alleging that Hus had been wrongfully judged a heretic. The nobility and many urban and rural Hussites rallied to the side of the dissenters. The alliance between Hussite dissent and Czech nationalism was temporarily sealed.

The burning of Hus, an intellectual, moderate reformist, enraged wide sections of the Czech population and encouraged the growth of cruder and more radical beliefs. A large proportion of the priests in Bohemia were now Hussites and spread the word through urban and rural parishes. Some of the priests became extremists, destroying images, renouncing the sacrificial priesthood, asserting the equality of Christians, and celebrating the Eucharist in barns and fields.

Increasing extremism, especially in the countryside, caused a sharper rift between the radicals and the moderates. The moderates rallied around Utraquism, because the Council of Constance had condemned Utraquism along with Hus, and adopted it as part of their rejection of the council. By rejecting the council, the Hussites implied the rejection of Apostolic Succession, which in effect left the Bible as the sole authority in the church. The Hussites proceeded to compel all the Bohemian clergy to administer the sacrament in both kinds, further undermining clerical authority in general, for reluctant priests were forced either to offer the chalice or to resign.

By 1417, the differences between the moderate, intellectual, urban clergy on the one hand and the rural radicals on the other were intensifying. Some radicals were already advocating the following: the whole Eucharistic service in Czech; the replacement of the Eucharistic sacrifice by a memorial Lord's Supper: Christians gathering together around the table to share the memorial meal. This meant the priesthood of all believers: anyone, lay or clerical, could say the Eucharistic prayers. The radicals also rejected purgatory, intercession by saints, infant baptism, images and relics, and confession to priests. They upheld the reading and interpretation of the Bible by individual laypersons under the illumination of the Holy Spirit. They denied the spiritual authority of priests or professors in the interpretation of Scripture. But they also promoted Scripture study groups with leaders who eventually assumed authority of their own.

By 1418, these radicals and the clerical, professorial moderates had little in common except their opposition to traditional Catholic orthodoxy and to temporal authorities attempting to legislate it. Efforts to bring the dissenting parties together failed, and at the 1418 synod at Prague the moderates condemned the denial of purgatory, lay consecration of the Eucharist, the destruction of images, the denial of infant baptism, and the rejection of the sacrificial priesthood. Above all, they declared that no novelty of belief or worship could be accepted without the approval of a synod composed of priests and professors.

The synod was unacceptable to radicals, and the movement might have disintegrated immediately had it not been for the helping hand of its opponents. In 1419, Wenceslas determined to suppress Hussitism in general, including both the radicals and the moderate Utraquists. This at once promoted Hussite unity and increased the influence of the radicals. Hussites were expelled from clerical office, sometimes with violence that engendered counter-violence. But preachers from the university had gone out and converted large numbers of countrypeople, who backed the radical cause.

Hussites, particularly in the countryside of southern Bohemia, now took up arms. A hill in that region, renamed Mount Tabor after the biblical mount of the transfiguration, became the rallying point for radical dissenters, the "Taborites." Taborite teaching is first known in its condemnation by the September 1418 synod of Prague. Its views, which set God and the Bible against the hierarchy, the sacraments, and Satan, spread through most of the countryside and eventually back into the cities. For the first time with the Taborites and their successors the Bohemian Brethren, a movement of dissent turned into a popular revolution, a pattern more typical of the Protestant Reformation than of the Middle Ages.

In Prague, the radicals were led by Jan Želivský, a regular canon influenced by Nicholas of Dresden and by Jakoubek. Linking the urban radicals with the Taborites, Želivský proclaimed that the faithful of Christ must wage war against the Antichrist represented by the pope and the king. The violence inherent in Joachist millenarianism, which proclaimed the final struggle between good and evil, Christ and Antichrist, now came to the fore, displacing the evangelical teaching of nonviolence and passive resistance. Želivský seized the churches and the town hall of Prague, expelling conservative clergy and forcing Wenceslas to accept a city council composed of Hussites. Wenceslas's death in 1419 could have opened the door to a victory for dissent, but once again, as soon as external pressures were relieved, the movement fractured.

On the death of Wenceslas, the intellectuals and merchants who made up the backbone of the moderate party tried to sew together a compromise with King Sigismund in order to suppress the radicals, whose violence threatened the entire kingdom. Even Jakoubek believed that Želivský had gone too far. The moderates agreed to reject radical doctrines and to support the new king in exchange for Sigismund's acceptance of Utraquism and of majority Czech control of the Bohemian state and church. The king agreed, and even the German minority, which was particularly terrified of the Taborites' violent radicalism, supported the agreement. The moderates thus changed sociologically from sect to church and themselves became part of the structure of order, while the radicals found themselves at war with both Catholics and moderate Hussites.

Taborite resistance continued, with Jan Žižka, a member of the royal army who had turned radical, leading the armed struggle. In 1419, Sigismund easily persuaded Pope Martin V to declare a crusade. But again the pope and king snatched defeat from the jaws of victory, reuniting the Hussites by condemning them all equally.

Between 1419 and 1420 the moderates and radicals, drawn together by the threat of crusade, met at the university to try to work out a common stand. Želivský assumed the leadership, and in 1420 they issued a united declaration called the Four Articles of Prague, affirming Utraquism, the free preaching of the Gospels, the disendowment of the clergy, including pope and bishops, and the freedom of the Kingdom of Bohemia "from sin and slander," perhaps referring to political independence as well as moral purity.

The Articles in a sense represented a political treaty between two hostile Hussite factions united only in their hatred of the Catholic establishment. In this alliance, the Radicals, composed of both urban and rural (Taborite) elements, prevailed. They enjoyed initial success on the battlefield. During 1420 to 1421, Žižka led the Taborites to several victories over Sigismund. But the Radicals soon fell victim to overconfidence and used their military advantage to force the moderates to submit to an extreme theological and liturgical statement.

The Prague radicals were now under the leadership of Želivský and Nicholas of Pelhřimov, whom the Radicals illegally made archbishop of Prague without proper consecration, thus eroding apostolic succession, while the Taborite radicals were led by Martin Húska, a Taborite who participated in the illegal consecration. The Radicals demanded that all Hussites, including clergy and professors, agree that neither reason nor tradition, neither apostolic authority nor academic learning, had any authority, but only the written word of Scripture. This doctrine was inherently inconsistent, for the Radical leaders assumed their own reading of Scripture to be the only true one and thus established themselves as new authorities. The tension between dissent and order could never be avoided.

The Radicals insisted upon the denial of the Real Presence of Christ in the Eucharist and made of the Eucharist a memorial and an *agape* (loving common meal) rather than a sacrifice; the true body of Christ was in heaven, not in a piece of bread. The kingdom of God was realized in the community of the elect, who not only imitated but actually reconstituted the Apostolic Church. Being saved and under the direction of the Holy Spirit, they had no need to obey laws. Those who did not agree with their interpretation were tools of Satan and had to be exterminated. The millennium was at hand; they were the army of the just, and the Catholics *and* moderate Hussites who did not follow their leadership were minions of the Antichrist in his last vain effort to stop the triumph of the just.

The Taborite liturgy followed this theology in being radically different from either the Catholic or the Utraquist Eucharist. The Taborites recited the Lord's Prayer in Czech, sat round a bare table in a bare church (or elsewhere if a church was not available) and recited the words of the Last Supper in the vernacular. They took turns reading from the Scriptures, heard sermons, and sang in

Czech. This liturgy was a complete departure from the Eucharist as the Real Body of Christ and from the sacrificing priesthood.

In the struggle between dissent and order, there will always be a party of order and a party of dissent. A religion can hold together only when the parties are in creative tension. Sometimes the tension becomes too intense, and the segments break apart. Sometimes order predominates to the point of suffocating the Spirit; sometimes dissent predominates to the point of atomizing the community. In the 1420s in Bohemia, the Catholics attempted to suffocate freedom, and in so doing provoked and prolonged a destructive struggle. This in effect promoted the formation of an independent Hussite church. But from its inception, the Hussite church itself was also torn between order and dissent. These divisions were complicated. In one, theological, view, the moderates represented order and the radicals dissent. In another, more sociological view, it was the radicals who represented order, because it was they who attempted to enforce their views on the moderates, who, as the minority, were dissenters. The moderates had little chance of success, pinned between the Catholics on the one hand and the Radicals on the other. But the Radicals were also split—by the incoherence of their own teaching that proclaimed individual reading of Scripture as the highest authority and at the same time imposed their views as correct. This produced a third tension between order and dissent, within the Radical camp itself. The antinomian ideals that they proclaimed were inevitably carried to extremes by some whose sense of the Spirit within them was eccentric and uncontrolled. Thus appeared the Adamites, who believed that the Garden of Eden had been recreated and original innocence restored; they went naked and prayed, "Our Father who art *within us.*" The Radical leaders Žižka and Húska acted as the force of order by repressing this and other extremist views themselves.

The extremes of the Radicals drove the moderates into opposition yet again. The Prague clergy, academics, and merchants reasserted moderate views, driving Želivský from power. He was executed in 1422; Huska had already been burnt in 1421. A threeway war ensued among Catholics, Radicals, and Moderates. Sigismund invaded Bohemia again in 1422 under the banner of a new crusade (there were five "crusades" in all: 1420, 1421, 1422,

1427, and 1431). The opposition became less theological, more military.

Once again, the intolerable fragmentation of society drove the parties to the bargaining table. The merchants and nobles who controlled the economic resources of the nation demanded peace. The Moderates and Catholics met at the Council of Basel in 1433 and agreed that the chalice could be administered to the laity on a voluntary basis, that the clergy were to administer their property modestly and responsibly, and that the authority of the bishops was to be maintained. It was a settlement that gave the Radicals nothing. The Taborites under the militant priest Procop continued armed opposition until his death in 1434. The compromise of the Moderates at Basel and Procop's demise combined with the exhaustion of the population and the longing of its leaders for peace to lower Hussite resistance, and Sigismund was able to reestablish Catholic rule between 1436 and 1437. Hussitism gradually diminished, but it lasted into the sixteenth century when it merged with Protestantism.

8

Conclusion

Direct connections link late medieval heresy with Protestantism. The Lollards in England, the Hussites in Bohemia, and some Waldensians who made common cause with the Taborites, merged with the Reformation. Other connections were indirect. Often Protestantism did well in areas of Europe that had in the Middle Ages been heavily influenced by heresy: the Low Countries and the Rhineland, Bohemia, and southern France. A map overlay of Calvinist communities in France and of those areas earlier influenced by Catharism would show a remarkable degree of congruity. Whereas a direct human and a doctrinal connection linked the Lollards and the Hussites, the French Reformers held a vaguer, but still strong, tradition of anticlericalism or at least antipapalism.

Another kind of connection was the continuation of certain medieval heretical ideas and ideals. It has long been debated whether this indicates an actual survival and influence of medieval ideas or whether the Protestants, faced with similar problems, arrived at similar solutions. Both answers are correct, possibly the latter more than the former. The ideal of apostolic poverty, for example, is bound to arise perennially in Christianity whenever the New Testament is taken seriously. Movements based on such an ideal occurred in the early church, the medieval church, the Reformation churches, and modern churches. Apostolic poverty is a kind of archetypal ideal in Christianity requiring no cultural transmission. Other ideas, such as the emphasis upon the Antichrist and the identification of the Antichrist with actual world leaders, especially the pope, moved directly from medieval radical sources into Protestant thought. To a certain extent the Reformers read medieval writers; therefore, such ideas were within the common range of knowledge.

The growing power of secular authorities in Christendom provided both connection and contrast. Beginning in the fifteenth century, and inceasingly so in the sixteenth, inquisitions in certain areas such as central Italy and especially Spain became agents of national consolidation and identity. The other side of the coin was that nations such as the Netherlands and England used fear of "The Inquisition" to establish their Protestant identities.

Social patterns shifted markedly from the time of the Reformist dissenters through the late medieval Evangelicals to the Protestant Reformers. A literate laity, an often disaffected clergy, an emphasis upon the Bible, the dissemination of theological tracts (enormously increased after the invention and spread of printing in the late fifteenth century), the increase of commercial and intellectual contacts among regions, the independence of universities, the growth of both popular and princely nationalism, the disarray of papal and episcopal authority, the attack on episcopally guarded tradition in favor of strict adherence to Biblical text, were all social factors and theological trends that contributed first to the rise of the Hussite movement and later to the Protestant Reformation. The two movements also had in common a tendency toward disagreements and schisms between moderates and radicals of various persuasions.

An element new to the Reformation era was the discourse of humanism, which originated in Catholicism but eventually was as effective among Protestants. The humanists emphasized literacy, education in both divine and secular knowledge, and drawing upon education and the intellect to interpret the Bible and theology. By the end of the sixteenth century, humanistic discourse would dominate Protestant thought.

At the same time, theological continuity existed, not only between the medieval dissenters and the Protestants but also between the medieval Catholics and the Protestants. Anyone reading Luther and Calvin against a background of medieval scholasticism sees them not only as continuing scholastic methods and vocabulary but also as expressing views similar to, and often identical with, those of medieval theologians. The allegedly great differences between

Protestants and Catholics on free will, grace, and predestination, for example, shrink in significance once one realizes that these issues had been discussed frequently by medieval theologians, the majority of whom tended to adopt positions that Luther and Calvin would later maintain.

Witchcraft

Nowhere is this continuity in belief clearer than in the strange phenomenon of witchcraft. Witchcraft can be seen as simple sorcery in the ancient and early medieval periods, or as neopaganism in the modern world. From about 1350 to 1700, it was perceived as diabolatry, the worship of Satan. Whether witches actually existed—that is, whether anyone actually worshipped Satan—is debated by modern historians, and the question may never be finally answered. Like the "Free Spirit," witchcraft was largely an invention of inquisitors—and of later historians. It is clear that the *concept* of diabolical witchcraft not only existed but was immensely powerful. It is probable that some people did worship Satan (similar movements existed both in ancient and modern times), but that such practices were limited to a few. The erroneous conviction that large numbers of witches were engaged in a conspiracy to betray Christian society to the Devil was almost universal in the sixteenth and seventeenth centuries among academics, clergy, rulers, and other dominant groups as well as among the ignorant. This conviction, because of its irrational exaggeration and bizarre social expressions, has often been referred to as the witch craze. During its course, hundreds of thousands were accused and many executed.

One of the curiosities of the witch craze is that the concept and idea of witchcraft passed unchanged from the Catholic fourteenth century into the Protestant sixteenth and seventeenth centuries, and that the prosecution of witches was equally strong in Catholic and Protestant regions; no significant statistical difference has been found. Some Catholic areas (such as Spain and Poland) were relatively immune, as were some Protestant regions (such as Prussia and Bohemia), but in France, western Germany, northern Italy, the Low Countries, England, and Switzerland the craze spread equally among Catholics and Protestants. Diabolical witchcraft consisted of a number of standard elements—the ride by night;

the pact with the Devil; the formal repudiation of Christianity; the secret, nocturnal meeting; the desecration of the Eucharist and the crucifix; the sexual orgy; sacrificial infanticide; and cannibalism. The roots of these concepts are found in ancient sorcery, pagan religion, and folklore. They are also found in medieval heresy.

Witchcraft was connected to medieval heresy in two ways. First, there is a conceptual similarity and possible direct influence between witchcraft and certain heretical ideas, such as antinomianism, antisacramentalism, and repudiation of the crucifix. More important, witchcraft was linked to heresy by judicial procedure. Indeed, witchcraft *became* a heresy when, beginning in the fourteenth and fifteenth centuries, authorities defined witches as the worst of all possible heretics for worshipping Christ's mightiest opponent.

Witches were therefore subject to the same judicial treatment as heretics: prosecution by local ecclesiastical courts, papal investigators, princes, and even urban and other local authorities both spiritual and temporal. Such prosecution, which began in the thirteenth century, gradually turned into a craze, the turning point being the years from 1484 to 1500. In 1484, Pope Innocent VIII issued the decree *Summis desiderantes affectibus* condemning witchcraft as heresy. In 1486, a learned book containing all "knowledge" about witchcraft and proclaiming its intent to conquer Christendom, the *Malleus maleficarum* (*The Hammer of Witches*), was published and printed. More copies of the *Malleus* were printed from 1486 through the first decades of the sixteenth century than of any other book save the Bible—an ironic comment on the moral effect of the invention of printing. The *Malleus* promoted misogyny—women were perceived in the later Middle Ages as more prone than men to heresy—as well as hatred of minorities and an irrational terror of secret plots. The assimilation of witchcraft to heresy marks almost as much of a change from the traditional medieval pattern of creative tension between dissent and order as the religious wars of the fifteenth and sixteenth centuries.

The argument of this book is that tension between dissent and order has existed throughout Christian history down to the present. This tension is an inevitable and necessary part of any system that endures for any significant length of time. If order is overemphasized, suffocation results; if dissent is overemphasized, fragmentation and atomization follow. The tension can be destructive and violent if perspective is lost. Yet if the guardians of order and the partisans of dissent operate with regard for the opinions of others and with the realization that every worldview, including one's own, is precarious, the ideology or the institution not only survives, but grows stronger. At times, the church has incorporated heterodox teachings, opening up to movements such as apostolic poverty; sometimes heresies have delayed orthodox acceptance of new practices, such as the laity's right to receive both the consecrated bread and the blood. Creative tension is the process by which the wisdom of tradition combines with the potentiality provided by new ideas and new ways. The only alternatives to creative tension are mindless reaction and equally mindless revolution.

For Christianity itself, the tension, though often destructive, has on the whole nourished theology and liturgy, forcing order to a degree of adaptation and dissent to a degree of unity. It has kept Christianity rooted in its origins and also alive, responsive to the Spirit and to the needs of contemporary people. Perhaps it is a way for the church to remain faithful to the spirit of Jesus, who was a revolutionary reformer yet at the same time a traditional Jew.

Document and Commentary

The alleged events at Orléans in 1022 illustrate the fundamental problem of dealing with original medieval sources, which tend to be sparse, biased, contradictory, sometimes written at a great distance in time or place from the events described, and from a worldview foreign to most modern scholars. Any book such as the present one is forced to make generalizations that may not be true. Exhibiting the trial of 1022 shows how tenuous some of the bases of our generalizations are.[14]

The first execution for heresy in the Middle Ages occurred at Orléans in 1022. This event has been subject to a wide range of interpretations from its first chroniclers down to the present. Twelve sources exist for the incident; eight are significant.[15] They differ both generally and in detail, so that no firm reconstruction of the events is possible. The earliest accounts by John of Ripoll (1023) and Adhémar de Chabannes (1028) are valuable but terse. The fullest, but not necessarily the most reliable, is by Paul de Saint-Père de Chartres (1078). Excerpts follow from a translation by Walter Wakefield.[16]

Paul focuses on the agent provocateur Aréfast, whom he claims to have known:

> This aforementioned Aréfast, by divine aid and by the keenness of his own healthy wit, not only detected but entirely suppressed in the city of Orléans the heretical

depravity which at that time was secretly spreading and pouring the poison of wicked error throughout the Gallic lands. He was of the lineage of the dukes of Normandy, a man refined in speech, wise in counsel, blessed with good habits, and therefore very well known for his services as emissary, not only to the king of the French but also among the great nobles. It is told that he had in his household at that time a certain cleric named Heribert, who for the purposes of study had decided to go to Orléans. But, in fact, while busily seeking authors of truth, he strayed down a blind path into a pit of flagrant heresy. . . . Two clerics, Stephen and Lisoius [a canon of the Church of the Holy Cross at Orléans] were in popular repute distinguished above all others in wisdom. . . . [Heribert] sought them out and after a brief interval, now become a docile disciple by the sweetness of the holy word, he was made drunken by them with deadly draughts of evil. Ensnared in madness and devilish error, lacking all knowledge of theology, he believed himself to have ascended the peak of wisdom. Returning to his homeland, he sought by gradual and subtle suggestion to draw his master [Aréfast] . . . with him into the path of error . . . His master . . . quickly informed Duke Richard [II of Normandy] of the situation, asked that the latter disclose to King Robert the [plague] then lurking in his kingdom, before it could spread, and requested that the king not refuse needful assistance to this same Aréfast in driving it out. [Aréfast went to Orléans and asked the advice of] a certain wise cleric named Evrard, sacristan of the church of Chartres. . . . [Aréfast went to the dissenters' meetings with the intent of disclosing their secrets to the authorities. Among other things he learned that] they said that Christ was not born of the Virgin, nor did He suffer for men, nor was He truly laid in the tomb, nor did He arise from the dead; and they added that in baptism there was no cleansing of sins, nor was there a sacrament [*sic*: should be translated *ritual*] in the consecration by a priest of the body and blood of Christ. They held for naught the invocation of holy martyrs and confessors. [Aréfast then asked them what really is to be believed, and they replied that they would cleanse his soul] by the imposition of our hands [and that] the gift of the Holy Spirit . . . will teach you without reserve the profundity and divine excellence of all the Scriptures. [The account went on to describe a Satanic orgy, interesting for the history of diabology but almost certainly a misrepresentation of this group. At length the group was taken in chains before the king and bishops, Aréfast among them, and Aréfast quickly exonerated himself by declaring himself a loyal vassal of Duke Richard and revealing what he claimed to have learned from the dissenters. The bishops then confronted Stephen and Lisoius, the leaders of the group, and asked them whether what Aréfast had said were true.] These men, for whom an abode in hell with the devil was already waiting, declared the enumerated articles to be true. . . . [After discussion and interrogation, they held to their beliefs, saying to the bishops] "You may spin stories in that way to those who have earthly wisdom and believe the fictions of carnal men, scribbled on animal skins. To us, however, who have the law written upon the heart by the Holy Spirit . . . in vain you spin out superfluities and things inconsistent with the Divinity." [On the same day most of the heretics were burnt.]

The difficulty of establishing "what really happened" is patent. Aréfast's betrayal of his acquaintances must have been tainted by exaggeration and fabrication. All the sources use vague rhetoric about demons, plagues, and insanity, standard tags for heresies among the fathers, and their use may indicate growing literacy and knowledge of the fathers on the part of these ecclesiastical writers. The story of the demonic orgy must be a false interpolation by Paul. The sources all agree that real heresy occurred, and the position taken by some historians that the dissenters were persecuted chiefly for political reasons cannot be sustained.

The sources indicate that the heretics may well have denied the Trinity, the creation of the world by God, the Incarnation, the Eucharist, penance, baptism, the prayers of the saints, the priesthood, and marriage as a sacrament. They emphasized the importance of inspiration by the Holy Spirit. They seem on the whole to have been an informal group holding Reformist ideas based on internal illumination and under the influence of charismatic figures. The group was characterized by a close relationship between the canons and laypeople. They were certainly not Cathars, as one modern writer imagined from the mention of imposition of hands in one document—a practice that goes back to the early church. R. I. Moore and Thomas Head have demonstrated considerable and complex political contamination of the proceedings.[17] The sources are in disarray over the political situation. Appeal to a secular authority (the king) was no proof in itself of secular contamination. From the time of Charlemagne, and beyond him back to late imperial Roman legislation, secular power was responsible for the repression of heresies.

Part of the political problem was a longstanding animosity. On the one side was Bishop Thierry of Orléans, supported by his ally Queen Constance, whose chaplain Stephen was a member of the heretical group of canons at Sainte-Croix, and on the other side was Thierry's enemy and successor Bishop Odolric. The king and queen supported Thierry as an ally in their effort to bring the Orléannais under closer royal power, but whatever their machinations toward the heretics were, they backfired, for Odolric became bishop and pressed the prosecution of the heretics, forcing Robert to condone the execution of persons with connections to the royal family. Head remarks that the trial was a political disaster for the king. Head also discusses other political dimensions too complex to introduce here. All in all the Orléans case is a microcosm of the difficulty of studying medieval dissent: the sources are few, they are contaminated, they are often contradictory, and they attract a variety of interpretations from modern historians—none of whom can ever obtain the whole truth.

Chronology

150–451: Gnosticism and Manicheism, dualist heresies; Montanism, Donatism, and Pelagianism, moral heresies; Arianism, Nestorianism, Monophysitism, Adoptionism, Christological heresies; Theodosian Code (438) makes heresy a crime; Council of Chalcedon (451) sets basic Christian theology.

451–700: Possibly Apocalyptic heretics described by Gregory of Tours (c. 590).

700–800: Aldebert, Clement, and Vergil: eccentric heretics; Iconoclasm, the doctrine that images were to be suppressed; Second Ecumenical Council of Nicea (787) condemns Iconoclasm; Charlemagne muddles the Iconoclastic issue at the Council of Frankfurt (794).

800–900: Amalarius of Metz condemned for arguing that the Eucharist was merely allegorical (838); Theuda, woman charismatic leader (847/8); Hincmar, Paschasius Radbert, Raban Maur, and Gottschalk debate predestination and the Eucharist; Eriugena (d. 877; cond. 855–859): a philosopher who was posthumously condemned for pantheism.

900–1000: Bogomils, dualist Bulgarian heretics (c. 915 on) who later influenced the Cathars.

1000–1050: The complicated heresy at Orléans (1022)

1050–1100: The Pataria (c. 1050–1075): the first mixing of urban politics with heresy; Berengar of Tours (d. 1088), an intellectual, disputes the nature of the Eucharist; Reverse heretics such as Simoniacs and Nicolaitists (c. 1075).

1100–1150: Peter Abelard (cond. 1121, 1140), an intellectual falsely condemned for heresy; Arnold of Brescia (cond. 1139; at Rome to 1155) leads a political and heretical revolt in Italy; Gratian's *Decretum* (c. 1140) sets pattern for canon (church) law against heresy; Cathars, the powerful Western dualist heresy from c. 1140; Peter of Bruys (d. c. 1140), Henry of Lausanne (d. c. 1145), and Eudo (c. 1145–48): popular wandering preachers.

1150–1200: Nicetas imports extreme dualist Dragovitsa rite (1160s) to the West; Cologne (1163) shows Cathar influence; Valdes, Reformist heretic and founder of the Waldensians (cond. 1179); Third Lateran Council (1179) sets stricter canon law controls on heresy; Council of Verona and decree *Ad abolendam* by Lucius III (1184) set pattern for future cooperation between temporal and spiritual authorities against heresy; first major Massacre of Jews, at York (1190); Innocent III, *Vergentis in senium* (1199), decree against heresy.

1200–1250: Joachim of Fiore (or his followers), *Liber figurarum* (c. 1200), the most influential apocalyptic book; Waldensians split into Lyonists and Poor Lombards (1205); Durand of Huesca renounces Waldensianism (1207) and becomes a leading Catholic preacher against the Cathars; Albigensian Crusade (1208–28); Franciscans founded (1209); Fourth Lateran Council (1215) issues stern prohibition of both heresy and new religious orders; Dominicans founded (1216); Conrad of Marburg (1227–33), first important papal inquisitor; Louis IX, decree *Cupientes* (1229) and Frederick II, *Liber augustalis* (1231), examples of strong secular legislation against heresy; Mass executions for heresy in Italy begin (1233); Massacre of Cathars at Montségur (1244); Peter John Olivi (c. 1248–1298), leader of Spiritual Franciscans, influenced by Apocalyptic thought.

1250–1300: Innocent IV, bulls *Ad extirpanda* (1252) and *Ad negotium* (1254), strong decrees against heresy by a canon lawyer pope; Gerard of Borgo San Donnino, *Eternal Gospel* (1254), a strongly Apocalyptic book; Gerardo Segarelli founds Apostolic Brethren (1260, burnt 1300); first Flagellant outbreak (1260); condemnations of theological propositions at University of Paris by Etienne Tempier (1269, 1270, 1277); Guglielma of Milan (d. 1281), female charismatic leader; Dolcino's manifesto for the Apostolici (1300): heretical melding of apocalyptic thought with ideal of poverty.

1300–1350: Marguerite Porete of Hainaut, author of a condemned book of spirituality (1306–1308); subsequent rise of Spiritual heresies; Council of Vienne decree *Ad nostrum* (1312) helps create image of nonexistent sect of the Free Spirit; John XXII, *Ratio recta* (1318), *Cum inter nonnullos* (1323), and other decrees from a pope hostile to the Spiritual movement; Bernard Gui, *Practica officii inquisitionis heretice pravitatis* (1322–24), influential manual for inquisitors; John XXII, *In agro dominico*, condemns Meister Eckhart (1329); widespread massacres of Jews (1348–50).

1350–1400: Beginnings of Bohemian Reform Movement (c. 1360); Jan Milič (c. 1363–73), Conrad Waldhauser, chaplain to Charles IV (1363–69), and Jan Hus (1372–1415) among the early leaders of the Bohemian Reform Movement; Lollards (c. 1380–c. 1520), popular movement in England following John Wyclif's teachings; English Bible (c. 1380–1400); Wyclif's *Confession* (1381); Archbishop William Courtenay's Blackfriars' Synod against Wyclif (1382).

1400–1450: *De haeretico comburendo* (1401), English secular legislation against heresy; Jan Hus named Dean of Philosophy at Prague (1401) and Rector of University of·

Prague (1409); Nicholas of Dresden's extreme Hussite treatise *Tabule veteris et novi coloris* (1412); Oldcastle's revolt (1413–14) linked to Lollards; Jakoubek of Stříbro and Utraquism (the doctrine that both the bread and wine must be given during communion [1412–20]); Hus's *De ecclesia* (1413), his most important statement on the nature of the church; Hus burnt at Council of Constance (1415); Taborites (1419 on), extreme rural Hussites; Imperial/papal Crusades against Hussites (1420, 1421, 1422, 1427, 1431); Jan Žižka defeats King Sigismund (1422); Procop the Shaven's military expeditions (1426–34); Ecumenical Council of Basel (1433).

1450–1500:   Innocent VIII, *Summis desiderantes affectibus* (1484), bull against witchcraft; *Malleus maleficarum* (1485/6), influential book against witchcraft; Prosecutions for Lollardy increase after 1486.

Notes and References

1. Ecumenical refers to the entire church; an ecumenical council is theoretically a gathering of all the bishops of the church.

2. Henry Charles Lea, *History of the Inquisition of the Middle Ages* (New York: Harper, 1887); J. B. Bury, *History of the Freedom of Thought* (London: Butterworth, 1913).

3. Otto Rahn, *Kreuzzug gegen den Graal* (Freiburg-im-Breisgau: Urbanverlag, 1933); Karl Kautsky, *Die Vorläufer des neueren Sozialismus* (Stuttgart: Dietz, 1895); Raoul Manselli, *Il secolo XII: Religione popolare ed eresia*, 2nd ed. (Rome: Jouvence, 1983).

4. Gregory of Tours, *History of the Franks*, 9:6; 10:25 and the prefaces to most of the "books".

5. Gary Macy, *The Theologies of the Eucharist in the Early Scholastic Period* (Oxford: Clarendon, 1984), 18–43 and passim, provides a thorough and sophisticated treatment of the question.

6. See the Document and Commentary.

7. Macy, 35–43.

8. Conservative views, because the requirements of clerical participation in a wedding and emphasis on private confession were orthodox innovations of that century.

9. H. A. Kelly, "Inquisition and Prosecution of Heresy: Misconceptions and Abuses," *Church History*, 58 (1989): 440. The Congregation of the Inquisition or Holy Office was established by Pope Paul IV in 1542. In 1965, Pope Paul VI reconstituted it as the Congregation for the Teaching of the Faith.

10. Joachim's most significant writings were the *Concordia*, the *Expositio in Apocalypsim*, and the *Psalterium decem chordarum*.

11. The measurement of the Ages differed: the Age of the Father went from Adam to Uzziah or from Adam to Christ; the Age of the Son from Uzziah to Benedict of Nursia or from Christ to the advent of the Spirit to come, and the Age of the Spirit from Benedict of Nursia on or from an unspecified projected later date (such as 1260). See Richard Emmerson, *Antichrist in the Middle Ages* (Seattle: University of Washington Press, 1981).

12. The usual terms are beguines for females and beghards for males. I follow Malcolm Lambert, *Medieval Heresy* (London: Arnold, 1977), in substituting the gender-neutral term beguin for both.

13. Most importantly *De ente* (1365–72), a realist philosophical treatise; *Postilla super totam bibliam* (1375–76), a commentary on the entire Bible; *De civili dominio* (1375–77), an attack on church property; *De ecclesia* (1377), defining Wyclif's view of the structure of the church; *De eucharista* (1379), a denial of transubstantiation; the "Confession" of 1381 and the *De blasphemia* (1381) against the peasants' revolt.

14. Most medieval sources for heresy are in Latin. The following are some useful collections in translation: *Visions of the End: Apocalyptic Traditions in the Middle Ages* (New York: Columbia University Press, 1979); Edward Peters, *Heresy and Authority in Medieval Europe* (Philadelphia: University of Pennsylvania Press, 1980); Jeffrey B. Russell, *Religious Dissent in the Middle Ages* (New York: John Wiley & Sons, 1971); and above all, Walter Wakefield and Austin P. Evans, *Heresies of the High Middle Ages* (New York: Columbia University Press, 1969).

15. Here are the eight most significant documents according to Thomas Head in his masterful article "Ascetic Circles in the Orleannais: Aristocratic Ambition and Religious Dissent in the Early Eleventh Century," in press. See also Head's *Hagiography and the Cult of Saints: The Diocese of Orleans, 800–1200,* (New York: Cambridge University Press, 1990).

(1.) John of Ripoll, *Letter of Abbot Oliba* in Andrew of Fleury, *Vie de Gauzlin, abbé de Fleury; Vita Gauzlini abbatis Floriacensis monasterii,* ed. and trans. Robert-Henri Bautier and Gillette Labory, *Sources d'histoire médiévale publiées par l'Institut de Recherche et d'Histoire des Textes,* 2 (Paris, 1969), 180–83. This text was composed in 1023.

(2.) Adhemar de Chabannes, *Chronicon,* ed. Jules Chavanon, *Collection pour servir à l'étude et à l'enseignement de l'histoire,* 20 (Paris, 1897), 184–85. This text was composed in its final form around 1028.

(3.) Andrew of Fleury, *Vita Gauzlini,* 96–103. Composed about 1042.

(4.) Andrew of Fleury, *Miracula Sancti Benedicti* in *Les miracles de*

Saint Benoît écrits par Adrévald, Aimoin, André, Raoul Tortaire et Hugues de Sainte Marie moines de Fleury, ed. Eugène de Certain (Paris, 1858), 246–48. Composed 1042–43.

(5.) Radulfus Glaber, *Quinque libri historiarum,* ed. John France (Oxford medieval texts, 1989), 138–51. Composed between 1046 and 1049.

(6.) Paul of Saint-Père de Chartres, *Cartulaire de l'abbaye de Saint-Père de Chartres,* ed. B. Guérard, 2 vols. *Collection des cartulaires de France,* 1 and 2 (Paris, 1840), 1:108–115. Composed after 1078.

(7.) *Vita Sancti Theoderici,* c. 4 in *Acta Sanctorum Ordinis Sancti Benedicti,* 6.1, 195–96. Composed in the late eleventh century.

(8.) *Chronique de Saint-Pierre-le-Vif de Sens, dite de Clarius,* ed. and trans. Robert-Henri Bautier and Monique Gilles, *Sources d'histoire publiées par l'Institut de Recherche et d'Histoire des Textes,* 3 (Paris, 1979), 114–15. Composed about 1110.

16. From Evans and Wakefield, op. cit., by kind permission of Walter Wakefield and of Columbia University Press.

17. Recent studies of these events include Head and also R. I. Moore, *The Formation of a Persecuting Society* (Oxford: Oxford University Press, 1987). I am indebted to both of these colleagues for their discussion of the subject. See also Robert-Henri Bautier, "L'hérésie d'Orléans et le mouvement intellectuel au début du XIe siècle: Documents et hypothèses," *Enseignement et vie intellectuelle,* Actes du 95e Congrès national des sociétés savantes: Section de philosophie et d'histoire jusqu'à 1610 (Paris, 1975): 1:63–88.

Bibliographic Essay

Historical understanding of the tension between dissent and order until the twentieth century was usually split between Catholic and Protestant. Throughout the twentieth century a variety of views have proliferated. Rather than narrowing in upon "the truth," we appear to be opening outward in our understanding toward a diversity of angles of vision. The best historians have drawn upon and expanded what had been good in earlier writings: they continue to prepare careful editions and analyses of original texts, and they are producing new interpretations by shining a variety of new methodological lights upon the texts.

The first great synthetic work of the twentieth century on dissent was Herbert Grundmann's *Religiöse Bewegungen im Mittelalter* (Berlin: Ebering, 1935; 2d ed., Hildesheim: Olms, 1961). Another important synthesis was Grundmann's *Ketzergeschichte des Mittelalters* (Gottingen: Vandenhoeck and Ruprecht, 1963). The most recent was Malcolm Lambert's *Medieval Heresy* (London: Arnold, 1977; 2d ed. in press). Lambert mistakenly defended the transmission of eastern dualism into the West before the 1140s and overemphasized the intellectual as opposed to political elements in the Wycliffite and Hussite movements. On the other hand, he correctly recognized the continuity in medieval heresy from the eighth through the fifteenth centuries, although he missed its connection with the Reformation. His was the most successful, thorough, and lucid effort to describe the entire span of medieval heresy since Lea's work in the previous century. And Lambert understood dissent as a genuinely religious phenomenon rather than translating it into modern secularist terms. Marxist interpretations of heresy as a whole were produced in Communist countries after World War II, such as Martin Erbstösser's *Heretics in the Middle Ages* (trans. Janet Fraser; Leipzig: Edition Leipzig, 1984; Orig.: *Ketzer im Mittelalter*, Stuttgart: Kohlhammer, 1984).

The variety of medieval views of heresy was explored in the book edited by W. Lourdaux and D. Verhelst, *The Concept of Heresy in the Middle Ages* (Louvain: Louvain University Press, 1976). Heresy in the early Middle Ages was first treated by Jeffrey B. Russell, *Dissent and Reform in the Early Middle Ages* (Berkeley: University of California Press, 1965) and R. I. Moore, *The Origins of European Dissent* (Oxford: Blackwell, 1977). Norman Cohn offered a peculiar but stimulating account linking medieval heresy to Marxism in *The Pursuit of the Millenium* (2nd ed., New York: Oxford, 1970). Brian Stock, himself not a heresiographer, in *The Implications of Literacy* (Princeton, N.J.: Princeton University Press, 1983) added to our understanding of early heresy with his notion of dissenting groups as "textual communities." H. M. M. J. Thijssen has recently contributed to our understanding of the way intellectual heresy fit into medieval thought in his forthcoming article, "Academic Heresies at the University of Paris: Controversies over Authority."

On the Waldensians, the most important works are Kurt-Viktor Selge, *Die ersten Waldenser, mit Edition des Liber antiheresis des Durandus von Osca [Huesca]* (Berlin: De Gruyter, 1967) and Giovanni Gonnet, *Les Vaudois au moyen âge* (with Amedeo Molnar; Turin: Claudiana, 1975).

On the Cathars, the leading writers have been Arno Borst, *Die Katharer* (Stuttgart: Hiersemann, 1953), Jean Duvernoy, *L'histoire des cathares* (Toulouse: Privat, 1979), René Nelli, *Spiritualité d'une hérésie: Le catharisme* (New York: AMS, 1980), Christine Thouzellier, *Catharisme et valdéisme en Languedoc à la fin du XIIe et au début du XIIIe siècle*, 2d ed. (Paris: Béatrice–Nauwelaerts, 1969), and Raoul Manselli, *L'eresia del male* (2d ed., Naples: Morano, 1980). Walter Wakefield's *Heresy, Crusade, and Inquisition in Southern France 1100–1250* (Berkeley: University of California Press, 1974) is the best account of the repression of the Cathars to date. Bernard Hamilton's *Monastic Reform, Catharism, and the Crusades, 900–1300* (London: Variorum Reprints, 1979) includes essays on Catharism in which he argued that Bogomil dualism became radical shortly before 1172 and therefore shortly before Nicetas's mission to the west.

Among the works on Joachim and millenarianism are E. Randolph Daniel, ed., *Abbot Joachim of Fiore: Liber de concordia novi ac veteris testamenti* (Philadelphia: American Philosophical Society, 1983), and Richard Emmerson, *Antichrist in the Middle Ages: A Study of Medieval*

Apocalypticism, Art, and Literature (Seattle: University of Washington, 1984). Bernard McGinn's study *The Calabrian Abbot: Joachim of Fiore in the History of Western Thought* (New York: Macmillan, 1985) vies with Marjorie Reeves's *Joachim of Fiore and the Prophetic Future* (London: S. P. C. K., 1976) and her *The Influence of Prophecy in the Later Middle Ages* (New York: Oxford University Press, 1969) as the foremost study. In *The Influence*, Reeves succeeded in drawing the focus of attention away from hoary debates over whether Joachim was orthodox to an examination of his enormously complex ideas and how they were adapted in an almost infinite set of permutations by his followers and by other writers both orthodox and heretical. In *Joachim of Fiore*, she concentrated on his historical vision and its influence through the seventeenth century. She warned us carefully, as did McGinn, of the complexity and inconsistency of Joachim's patterns, which encouraged a diversity of interpretations by those drawing from him as well as misunderstandings by modern historians.

On the Franciscans, David Burr, *Olivi and Franciscan Poverty: Origins of the usus pauper Controversy* (Philadelphia: University of Pennsylvania Press, 1989) argued that despite differences, the factional division between conventuals and spirituals did not emerge until after 1300. He found that the division was created by the dispute over Olivi's *usus pauper* doctrine. Olivi died in 1298, but the division became fixed only after John XXII's intervention. Both Burr and Duncan Nimmo, *Reform and Division in the Medieval Franciscan Order: From St. Francis to the Foundation of the Capuchins* (Rome: Capuchin Historical Institute, 1987), found Olivi's interpretation of the *usus pauper* flexible and reasonable and the opposition to it rigid and intolerant.

The basic book on the Free Spirit is Robert Lerner's *The Heresy of the Free Spirit in the Later Middle Ages* (Berkeley: University of California Press, 1972), which showed conclusively that the heresy had never existed as an organized group except in the fantasy of the orthodox authorities. Further investigation into the process by which the forces of order created an imaginary heresy is needed, especially linking the process to the creation of the fiction of witchcraft. Some individuals did engage in some of the practices in question, but why and how they were fictionalized into a sect remains an important question.

For the Lollards, Anne Hudson is the foremost authority. Among her numerous works on Lollardy are *Lollards and Their Books* (London: Hambledon, 1985) and *The Premature Reformation: Wycliffite Texts and Lollard History* (New York: Oxford University Press, 1988), the culmination of 20 years of scholarship during which Hudson has revised our views of Lollardy, arguing that it was more a heresy of the scholars and gentry than of the lower classes. Additionally, she has provided, from deep research in the records, a remarkably clear view of how Lollards thought, worshiped, and behaved. Margaret Aston also illuminated the topic with the first volume of *England's Iconoclasts* (New York: Oxford University Press, 1988) and *Lollards and Reformers: Images and Literacy in Late Medieval Religion* (London: Hambledon, 1984). In the first volume of *England's Iconoclasts* entitled *Laws Against Images*, Aston argued that the "great shift of religious consciousness" in the English Reformation centered on images (idolatry, as the Protestants put it) and that this important shift was rooted in medieval Lollardy as well as in the earlier iconoclast controversy.

On the Hussites, the literature is vast, as the bibliography by Jarold Knox Zeman, *The Hussite Movement and the Reform in Bohemia, Moravia, and Slovakia (1350–1650)* (Ann Arbor: University of Michigan Press, 1977) shows, but the most accessible books in English remain Frederick Heymann's narrative *John Žižka and the Hussite Revolution* (Princeton, N.J.: Princeton University Press, 1955) and Howard Kaminsky's analytical *History of the Hussite Revolution* (Berkeley: University of California Press, 1967), which emphasizes the political and nationalist currents of the movement and the religious splits within the movement caused by these currents. Matthew Spinka, *John Hus: A Biography* (Princeton, N.J.: Princeton University Press, 1968) is still useful.

On witchcraft and magic there is Valerie Flint, *Religion and the Rise of Magic in Early Medieval Europe* (Princeton, N.J.: Princeton University Press, 1990), H. Ansgar Kelly, *The Devil, Demonology, and Witchcraft* (2d ed., New York: Doubleday, 1974), Edward Peters, *The Magician, the Witch, and the Law* (Philadelphia: University of Pennsylvania Press, 1978), Jeffrey B. Russell, *Witchcraft in the Middle Ages* (Ithaca: Cornell University Press, 1972), Richard Kieckhefer, *European Witch Trials: Their Foundations in Popular and Learned Culture, 1300–1500* (Berkeley: University of California Press, 1976), and Carlo Ginzburg, *Ecstasies: Decoding the Witches' Sabbath* (Berkeley: University of California Press, 1991). Kieckhefer's *Magic in the Middle Ages* (Cambridge: Cambridge University Press, 1989) distinguished between magic and witchcraft. Kieckhefer showed that terms such as magic and witchcraft are fuzzily bordered for both medieval and modern writers. The book also showed how medieval people mixed science, religion, and witchcraft indiscriminately and that the practitioners of this "magic" could be from a variety of groups and classes: priests, physicians, midwives, and ordinary people with folk memory of cures or curses.

On repression, the best and most accessible work includes James Given, "The Inquisitors of Languedoc and the Medieval Technology of

Power," *American Historical Review* 94 (1989): 336–59. He examines the underlying social and political structures that facilitated the work of the Inquisition in Languedoc during the thirteenth and fourteenth centuries. Between them, Edward Peters, *Inquisition* (New York: Free Press, 1988), and Henry Ansgar Kelly, "Inquisition and the Prosecution of Heresy, Misconceptions and Abuses," *Church History* 58 (1989): 439–51, overthrow the fallacy that there was ever a centrally organized inquisition or that inquisitions were primarily concerned with heresy.

On the Jews, see Bernard Bachrach, *Early Medieval Jewish Policy in Western Europe* (Minneapolis: University of Minnesota Press, 1977); Robert Chazan, *Dangers of Faith: Thirteenth-Century Christian Missionizing and Jewish Response* (Berkeley: University of California Press, 1989); and his *New Christian Missionizing of the Thirteenth Century* (Cambridge, Mass: Harvard University Press, 1988). Chazan argues a fundamental shift in the thirteenth century in the church's approach to Jews. From that time, the authorities used Hebrew and Arabic for missionary purposes; they sought to obtain royal decrees compelling Jews to attend Christian sermons and debates between Christians and Jews; and they deliberately developed proselytizing arguments based on Jewish exegetical traditions and haggadah. These changes sprang from the increasing self-confidence and organizational power of the church but also developed because the scholastic division of opinions into the rational and the irrational placed Judaism in the category of irrationality, and made Jewish refusal to accept Christianity seem a stubborn and willful refusal to accept rationally demonstrable truth. Gavin Langmuir contributed a theoretical study of antisemitism, *History, Religion, and Antisemitism* (Berkeley: University of California Press, 1990) and a collection of more historical essays, *Toward a Definition of Antisemitism* (Berkeley: University of California Press, 1991), which made an extremely useful distinction between nonrationalism on the one hand and the dichotomy between rational and irrational on the other. Langmuir showed how the shift from nonrational religion to rational theology inevitably defined some nonrational ideas as irrational and therefore heretical. As scholastic theologians defined the Eucharist in finer and more complex terms, doubts about transubstantiation increased during the thirteenth and fourteenth centuries, becoming explicit in the fifteenth. Christians, fearing the loss of their faith, projected this fear upon Jews and heretics and so intensified their persecution.

R. I. Moore's *The Formation of a Persecuting Society* (Oxford: Blackwell, 1987) took an important sociological perspective toward dissent by assimilating prosecution of heretics with that of Jews, lepers, homosexuals, and prostitutes. Moore's case was that Christian society first became a persecuting society in the eleventh and twelfth centuries when the clerical "elitists" that governed both the spiritual and temporal institutions of Western Christendom entered a crisis. Because the power of these "elites" controlled both the spiritual and temporal realms, it was not the "church" as such but "society" as a whole that experienced the crisis. Social and religious persecutions were linked in stereotyping and victimizing the marginal groups.

By the twelfth century, in Moore's argument, feeling their authority weakened or challenged by the rise of alternate power brokers such as urban commercial and industrial leaders, and weakening themselves by infighting, the "elites" consolidated their power by constructing a series of intellectual, legal, moral, political, and ecclesiastical definitions that fortified them within a thick wall of legitimacy. By building this wall, they necessarily and intentionally excluded some groups outside the wall, treating them as threats to Christendom.

Lately the idea is growing that dissent and order are part of the same story, and that there can be no history of heresy separate from its counterpart, orthodoxy. My own early work took a step in that direction, as did Moore's, and the present book makes this position more explicit and central.

In the late twentieth century, a truly large amount of new work—about 100 titles a year—continues to appear on medieval dissent. Predicting what new angles of vision the twenty-first century will produce would be rash, but their variety will point us gradually toward the truth, provided they include the following: a continued search for new documents relative to dissent; a review of already-known documents with an eye to seeing new implications for dissent; a use of new conceptual approaches to an understanding of dissent; a continued rootedness in the tradition of solid work already accomplished; an increased awareness of the multiplicity of lenses through which we seek to understand dissent and orthodoxy and the tension between them; a firm moral and loving commitment to the men and women of the past whose lives and thoughts are as real and as important as our own.

Index

"Dissent," definition of, 1
"Docetism," 13
Dolcino, 75–76
Dominicans, 58–63, 68
"Donatism," 6, 28, 84
Dragovitsa, Order of, 51
Drugonthia. See Dragovitsa
Dualism, 13, 16, 19, 42–43, 47–54, 114–15
Duns Scotus, 69
Durand of Huesca, 57
Duvernoy, Jean, 115

Eckhart, Meister, 79
"Ecumenical," 1, 10, 12
Edward I, King of England, 41, 72
Ekbert of Schönau, 49–50
Elizabeth of Schönau, 50
Emmerson, Richard, 115–16
Endura, 52
Erbstösser, Martin, 115
Erigena, John Scotus, 17–18, 65–66
Erlembald, 30–31
Eudo, 24
Everwin, 49
Evrard, sacristan of Church of Chartres, 104
Excommunicamus, 63
"Excommunication," 33, 46, 83, 90
Exivi de paradiso, 75, 78

Fathers of the Church, 2, 4, 13, 33, 36, 38, 45, 49, 86–87
  and apocalyptic thought, 14–15
  at Chalcedon, 6
Fidei catholicae fundamento, 75
Flagellants, 73
Flint, Valerie, 117
Four Articles of Prague, 94–95
Francis of Assisi, 37, 46, 58, 72, 74–75
Franciscans, 58, 63, 66, 73–75, 78, 116
Frankfort, Council of, 16
Fraticelli, 75, 78, 80
Frederick I, Emperor, 47
Frederick II, Emperor, 70, 75
"Free Spirit," 66, 73, 76–78, 100, 116

Garatenses, 51
Gerard of Borgo San Donnino, 73
Gerardo Segarelli, 73, 75
Gilbert de la Porrée, 37
Ginzburg, Carlo, 117
Given, James, 117–18
Gnosticism, 13, 19, 48–49
Gonnet, Giovanni, 115
Gottschalk, 17–18
Gratian, 23, 43, 47
Gregory of Tours, 15
Gregory VII, Pope, 3, 31
Gregory IX, Pope, 61–63
Gregory XII, Pope, 84
Grundmann, Herbert, 114
Guglielma of Milan, 76
Gundulf, 28

Hadrian I, Pope, 19
Hadrian IV, Pope, 35, 47
Hamilton, Bernard, 115
Hartmann, John, 78
Head, Thomas, 106
Henry II, King of England, 50
Henry V, King of England, 87
Henry of Lausanne, 32–35, 62
Henry of Marcy, Abbot of Clairvaux, 55
Henry of Virneburg, Archbishop of Cologne, 77, 79
"Heresiarch," 26, 34
"Heresy," definition of, 2
Heribert of Orleans, 104
"Heterodoxy," 2–3, 9, 12, 19, 21, 25, 30, 32, 36–37, 43, 47, 57, 60, 65, 76, 102
Heymann, Frederick, 117
"Hierarchy", 4, 28, 51–52, 84, 93
Hildebert of Lavardin, 32–33
Hildegard of Bingen, 50
Hincmar, Archbishop of Reims, 17–18
Honorius Augustodunensis, 87
Honorius III, Pope, 61
Hudson, Anne, 86, 116–17
Hugh of Digne, 66, 74
Hugh of Lincoln, 41
Humbert of Silva Candida, 3–4

The Author

Jeffrey Burton Russell (B.A. and M.A., University of California, Berkeley, Ph.D., Emory University) is a Fulbright Fellow (University of Liège), a Junior Fellow of Harvard University, a Guggenheim Fellow (Warburg Institute), a National Endowment for the Humanities Fellow, and a Fellow of the Medieval Academy. He published *Dissent and Reform: Heresy in the Early Middle Ages* (1965), *A History of Medieval Christianity* (1968), *Religious Dissent in the Middle Ages* (1971) and *A History of Medieval Witchcraft* (1972), before turning to his five-volume history of the idea of the Devil (*The Devil; Satan; Lucifer; Mephistopheles; The Prince of Darkness* [1977–88]). He edited *Medieval Heresies: A Bibliography 1960–1979* (1981), revealing that interest in heresy had produced more than 2,000 titles in those two decades. His most recent book is *Inventing the Flat Earth: Columbus and Modern Historians* (1991). Russell has taught at the University of New Mexico, UC Berkeley, Harvard, UC Riverside, the University of Notre Dame, and since 1979 at UC Santa Barbara, where he is cochairman of Medieval Studies.

The Editor

Michael S. Roth is the Hartley Burr Alexander Professor of Humanities at Scripps College and professor of history at the Claremont Graduate School. He is the author of *Psycho-Analysis as History: Negation and Freedom in Freud* (1987) and *Knowing and History: Appropriations of Hegal in 20th-Century France* (1988), both published by Cornell University Press. He is currently writing about contemporary strategies for representing the past in the humanities and about conceptualizations of memory disorders in the nineteenth century.